How Should Research be Organised?

How Should Research be Organised?

Donald Gillies

ISBN 978-1-904987-27-7

College Publications
Scientific Director: Dov Gabbay
Managing Director: Jane Spurr
Department of Computer Science
King's College London, Strand, London WC2R 2LS, UK

http://www.collegepublications.co.uk

Original cover design by Richard Fraser
Cover created by orchid creative   www.orchidcreative.co.uk
Printed by Lightning Source, Milton Keynes, UK

Table of Contents

Preface

The question: 'how should research be organised?' is one that is bound to be increasingly raised though out the world. In the last few decades, science and science-based technologies have entered more and more into the processes of production and distribution. We live in the age of computers and DNA. This means that any country which aspires to have a modern industrial base, must create its necessary complement – a research base. Now it is clearly desirable that such a research base should be organised so that a great deal of high quality research is produced by the funds that are put into it. But how is such a desirable outcome to be achieved? This question is by no means easy to answer.

The best approach to the question is to begin by examining some of the existing systems of research organisation, and by trying to find out their advantages and drawbacks. In this book I will concentrate mainly on systems of research organisation in the UK. This is partly of course because these are the systems most familiar to me, but I think that they are also of quite general interest. In 1986 a novel approach to research organisation in the UK was introduced by Thatcher in the form of what is called the **Research Assessment Exercise** (or **RAE**). Details of how this works are given in chapter 1. The RAE was continued by Blair and in fact has been used in the UK from 1986 to 2008. The RAE is based on what is known as **peer review**, and this is a component of many, if not most, systems of research organisation. This is one reason why an analysis of the RAE has a broad significance. Part 1 of the book gives a critique of the RAE. It is argued that the RAE is both very costly, and likely to reduce the quality of the research produced.

Whether for the same or different reasons, the UK government which supported the RAE for many years, seems now to have reached the conclusion that it is unsatisfactory. It has been announced that, from 2009, the RAE will be replaced by a system based on what are called: **metrics**. The most well-known metric is a **citation index**, which records how many times the papers of one researcher are cited by other researchers. Metrics, like peer reviews, are a feature of most systems of research organisation. Part 2 of the book gives a critique of the new metrics-based system. It is argued that it is certainly no better, and probably worse, than the RAE.

Parts 1 and 2 are the critical parts of the book. Part 3 attempts to be more constructive by putting forward a proposal for a new system of research organisation. It is argued that this alternative system would produce better quality research at a much lower cost than either the RAE or the system based on metrics.

As can be seen, there are quite a number of different ways in which research could be organised, and this raises the question of how we can test out these different approaches to find out which one is best. In the book I suggest (**5.2**) the use of **historical tests**. The idea is this. We naturally want our system of research organisation to encourage major research advances. Let us therefore consider some major such advances from the past, and see how the researchers who carried them out would have fared under the system under consideration. If they would have fared well, the system passes the test. If they would have fared badly, it fails the test and should be altered. The book applies this approach using a variety of examples of excellent research, taken from different fields. These include Einstein's discovery of Special Relativity (**9.3**), Fleming's discovery of penicillin (**10.3**), Frege's introduction of modern mathematical logic (**2.2**), and Wittgenstein's work on his masterpiece: *Philosophical Investigations* (**1.3**). It is shown that both the RAE and the metrics-based approach systematically fail these historical tests, and hence that they would, had they been in force at an earlier historical period, have held up, or even prevented altogether, the corresponding important research advances. The proposed alternative system outlined in Part 3 of the book, on the other hand, passes these historical tests with flying colours.

Donald Gillies
Professor of Philosophy of Science and Mathematics
Dept. of Science and Technology Studies, University College London
donald.gillies@ucl.ac.uk

November 2008

Acknowledgements

Much of the material in Part 1, Chapters 1-5 of the book is based on a talk which I gave at the Royal Institute of Philosophy, London in November 2005 as part of a series on Philosophy of Science organised by the Institute's director Professor Anthony O'Hear. This talk was later published in Anthony O'Hear (ed.), *Philosophy of Science. Royal Institute of Philosophy Supplement: 61*, Cambridge University Press, 2007, pp. 37-73. I would like to thank the Royal Institute of Philosophy and its director Anthony O'Hear for permission to reprint material from this article, and also for giving me the chance of presenting it to a critical audience whose comments were very helpful.

In Chapters 5, 7 & 8, I use material from a paper entitled: How should research be organised? An alternative to the UK research assessment exercise, which is forthcoming in 'From Knowledge to Wisdom: Studies in the Thought of Nicholas Maxwell', edited by Leemon McHenry (Ontos Verlag). I am very grateful for permission to use this material.

I would also like to give special thanks to my wife, Grazia Ietto Gillies, with whom I have discussed all the ideas in this book. I expound her suggestion for replacing **peer review** by **peer comment** in **9.6**. She has read through the final draft carefully, and offered very useful suggestions for improvements.

Part 1.

Critique of the Research Assessment Exercise (RAE)

Chapter 1. The Need for an Assessment of the Research Assessment Exercise

1.1 Introduction to the Research Assessment Exercise

The first part of this book is devoted to a critique of the UK's research assessment exercise (henceforth abbreviated to RAE). However, for readers unfamiliar with the RAE, it would be as well to begin by explaining how it works. The RAE was introduced in 1986 by Thatcher, and was continued by Blair. So it has now (i.e. in 2008) been running for 23 years. During this time, the rules governing the RAE have changed considerably, and the interval between successive RAEs has also varied. These changes are not of great importance as far as the arguments of this book are concerned. I will therefore concentrate on the main features of the RAE which can be summarised as follows.

At intervals of a few years, RAEs are carried out in all the universities of the UK. The first step is to appoint a committee of assessors in each subject. These assessors are usually academics working in the field in question in the UK. Next most members of each department in a subject have to select a set of pieces of their research. The department then submits all these pieces of research produced by its members to the assessment committee. The members of the committee study this research output, and, on its basis, grade the department on a scale running from very good downwards. The departments which score well on the RAE are provided with research funds. Those which don't score so well are less fortunate. They are provided with much smaller funds for research, and the members of such departments have to spend more time on teaching. Recently there have even been moves in some universities to close altogether departments which perform badly on the RAE.

Such then in rough outline is the procedure followed in the RAE. It should be pointed out that the RAE is a costly operation. First of all it involves a lot of work which has to be carried out by professional administrators. Very often universities have had to appoint extra administrative staff to deal with the volume of work generated by the RAE. Secondly, the extra work involved in the RAE takes up a great deal of academics' time which, in the absence of the RAE, could be spent on the more productive activities of research and teaching. As the time of academics also costs money, this too adds to the cost of the RAE. The question then naturally arises as to whether this expensive procedure has actually improved the research produced in the UK. Strange to say this question is rarely asked. Academics devote themselves with great energy to evaluating each other's work, but seem to be little concerned with evaluating an important government policy. Perhaps the reason for this is that it seems at first sight rather obvious that the RAE should improve the UK's research output. The procedure conforms to common sense. If we want to improve research, we should first find out who is doing good research and then give funding to the good researchers while withdrawing funding from the bad researchers. The RAE appears at first sight to be doing just this, and so the conclusion seems unavoidable that introducing such a system will improve research output.

In social life, however, things are rarely simple, and judgements based on common sense can often mislead. The very costly RAE is designed to improve the research output of the UK, but could it be having the opposite effect? Could it be making the research output of the UK worse instead of better? In the first part of this book I will argue that the RAE is indeed likely to have a negative effect on the research output of the UK. But how can we assess the research assessment exercise itself? An obvious procedure is to to choose a particular subject, and see whether the research output in that subject has improved since the RAE was introduced in 1986, or, on the contrary got worse. Most of this book will be concerned with examples from science which I will use in a broad sense to include computer science, mathematics and medicine, as well as the standard natural sciences such as astronomy, chemistry and physics. However, I do not want to neglect research in the humanities, whose importance is, in my view, very often underestimated. So I will begin by taking an example from the humanities, and consider whether the RAE has improved research in philosophy in the UK.

1.2 Has the RAE improved Philosophy in the UK?

Let us consider philosophy in the UK in the period 1900-1975, that is to say in the twentieth century but before the introduction of the RAE. This period of almost three quarters of a century was one of great brilliance as regards philosophy in the UK. It begins in the years before the First World War with the Cambridge school founded by Moore and Russell. Moore wrote an outstanding work on ethics while Russell made his remarkable contributions to logic and philosophy of mathematics. They were followed in the next generation by Keynes who was at this time still a philosopher rather than an economist, and who did important research in the philosophy of probability and induction. Wittgenstein also came to Cambridge in this period, and, working with Russell, he developed his early philosophy. After the First World War, philosophy continued to flourish at Cambridge. The prodigious Frank Ramsey died in 1930 at the age of only 26, but not before he made remarkable contributions to the philosophy of logic, probability and mathematics. In that same year, however, Wittgenstein obtained a post at

4

Cambridge where he remained with short interruptions until 1947, rising to the position of professor. It was during this period that Wittgenstein developed his later philosophy, and wrote most of his book: *Philosophical Investigations*. Wittgenstein died in 1951, and *Philosophical Investigations* was published posthumously in 1953. Many people regard this book as the greatest philosophical masterpiece of the twentieth century.

After the Second World War, in the period 1945-75, philosophy continued to flourish in the UK, but Cambridge was no longer the main centre. Instead this period is dominated by the ordinary language school of philosophy at Oxford, and by Popper's school in London. Ordinary language philosophy had much in common with Wittgenstein's later philosophy, but it was developed in a somewhat different way at Oxford by figures such as Ryle and Austin. Popper and his school focussed on philosophy of science. The school included not only Popper himself, but Lakatos, and, one might say, half Feyerabend. I say 'half Feyerabend' because Feyerabend started as Popper's assistant, and his first lectureship was in Bristol in the UK. However, he later worked in the USA and continental Europe. Still up to the death of Lakatos in 1974, Feyerabend visited London frequently giving regular lecture courses there.

The Oxford school and Popper's school were not on the best of terms. Their feud was foreshadowed by a famous argument between Popper and Wittgenstein which took place in 1946, and has become the subject of Edmonds and Eidinow's interesting 2001 book: *Wittgenstein's Poker*. However, a feud between two rival and very different schools of philosophy is surely yet another sign that philosophy was flourishing in the UK.

Moreover in the period 1945 to 1975, there were other significant developments in philosophy in the UK which lay somewhat outside the main schools just described. Perhaps the most important of these was the beginning of the philosophy of artificial intelligence. In his classic article published in *Mind* in 1950, Turing argued that computers could eventually equal if not surpass human beings in intellectual skills. Lucas replied in 1961 with a famous argument which used Gödel's incompleteness theorems to try to show that the human mind would always remain ahead of any possible computer.

So surveying philosophy in the UK in the years 1900-1975 one cannot but conclude that this was a brilliant period in which philosophy of the highest quality was produced in abundance in the UK. However, this was all before anyone had thought of introducing the RAE, and there was no system in operation which resembled the RAE in any way. Doesn't this begin to suggest that the RAE may be quite unnecessary?

At this point, however, a stern defender of the RAE might say: 'This is all very well, but there is never any good reason for being complacent. Even if things are going satisfactorily, there is still always room for improvement, and the RAE was designed to achieve such improvement.' Well, the RAE may have been designed to bring about improvement, but did it succeed? The RAE has been with us since 1986. Has the philosophical output of the UK improved during the years form 1986 to 2008?

Having formulated this last question, I have to confess that I am unable to answer it. I am genuinely unsure as to whether philosophy produced in the UK in the last 10 years say has been good or not. Naturally some pieces of UK philosophy have struck me as good, while others have appeared to me as quite bad. However, even these judgements I hold tentatively and with considerable uncertainty, while I am, at the same time, completely certain that others hold quite different opinions from mine about what is good and what is bad. Earlier I talked about philosophy in the period 1945 to 1975, and here I felt confident about the opinions I expressed. After the lapse of more than thirty years, a historical perspective has been obtained and it becomes easy to judge who were the important philosophers, and to evaluate the significance of their contributions. The situation is quite otherwise with contemporary philosophy where it is hard to say which philosophical works have a real importance, which are now esteemed only because of some passing fashion, and which are at present unjustly neglected because their true significance has not yet been grasped.

Just as I have been writing about philosophy in the UK in the period 1945 to 1975 which ended thirty years ago, let us imagine someone writing about the period 1986 to 2008 in the year 2040. Can we guess what such a writer might say? There could be a spectrum of judgement along a scale running from those most favourable to the RAE to those most hostile to it. A very favourable judgement might go like this: 'Although few realised it at the time, the year 1986 proved a turning point for philosophy in the UK. The introduction of the RAE in that year stimulated the philosophy community in the UK to greater efforts and we can now recognize that the works they produced in the subsequent decades outshone those completed in the first three quarters of the twentieth century.' A very hostile judgement might go like this: 'There was a brilliant flowering of philosophy in the UK in the first three quarters of the twentieth century. Unfortunately after about 1975, a decline set in and the situation was made worse by the introduction of the RAE in 1986. In the decades following this introduction, philosophy in the UK, which earlier in the century had been so brilliant, sank to a very low point.' These two judgements could be taken as marking the extreme points of a scale. Where along this scale will the majority of writers in 2040 be found? I really would not like to say.

6

One important point has emerged from the preceding discussion, namely that it is often very difficult to judge the quality of contemporary research. It is often only after the elapse of a considerable interval of time –say thirty years or more – that one can say with any confidence that a piece of research was either genuinely good or really very bad. The situation is indeed worse than this, for, as we shall see in the next chapter, contemporary judgements on the quality of pieces of research, are often wildly mistaken in the light of what emerges later on. But this exposes a key weakness in the RAE. The RAE naturally relies on contemporary judgements as to which researchers are good and which are bad, but such judgements are difficult to make and may often be found to be quite wrong in the light of later developments.

This point turns out to be crucial for many of the arguments which will be presented in this book, and I will return to it again and again. However, let us leave it for the moment, and return to the problem of assessing whether the effect of the RAE on philosophical output has been good or bad. As we have seen, the direct approach of asking whether the introduction of the RAE improved the quality of philosophy in the UK did not yield any very clear answer. This is why I suggest using another approach which could be called **the historical approach**. As we have seen, it is very difficult to say whether a piece of contemporary research is good or bad, and contemporary judgements on this question may be shown in the long run to be quite erroneous. On the other hand, once thirty or more years have elapsed, historical perspective has been obtained and it is then possible to judge with some confidence whether a piece of research was good or bad. So to assess the RAE and indeed other suggested systems for research organisation, we should focus on examples of research from the past. Of course the RAE, which was introduced in 1986, would not have existed at the time of such research. However, we can still ask whether, if the RAE had been in existence at that time, it would have improved that research or would, on the contrary, have made it worse. As we shall see when we consider particular examples, it is relatively easy to answer these questions in a convincing manner, and this provides a means of assessing the RAE.

As most of the examples which will be considered are drawn from science, this shows the relevance of history and philosophy of science to the problem of evaluating the RAE. We can explain this relevance in more general terms as follows. Let us begin with history of science. Historians of science study the great episodes of scientific advance, and the research programmes which led to exciting discoveries and to new and important knowledge. However, they also study the research programmes which failed to produce any advances, and the obstacles and difficulties which have sometimes stood in the way of scientific progress. All these matters are surely relevant to the design of a government policy intended to improve scientific research.

7

Moreover it is not just the individual episodes which are relevant. One needs to analyse the underlying general principles which favour scientific advance, or, conversely, the general nature of the obstacles which impede scientific progress. This task of generalising from history of science falls to the practitioners of philosophy of science. Thus I think there can be little doubt that history and philosophy of science is highly relevant to assessing the effectiveness of the RAE. However, as our first illustration, of how the historical approach can be applied to assessing the RAE, I will in the next section consider an example from the history of philosophy.

1.3 How would Wittgenstein have fared in the RAE?

Let us then apply our historical approach to philosophy in the UK in the 1930s. Suppose the RAE had been introduced in say 1936, what effect would it have had on philosophy in the UK? This was the time when Wittgenstein was developing his later philosophy at Cambridge and writing early drafts of what later became his *Philosophical Investigations*, judged by many to be the greatest philosophical book of the twentieth century. How would Wittgenstein have fared in a RAE conducted according to the standard rules?

Actually we can answer this question quite easily. Wittgenstein was offered a position at Cambridge in 1930, rose to becoming professor there, and resigned from his chair in 1947. During these 17 years he published nothing. In fact the last philosophical work which he published in his lifetime was a paper entitled: 'Some Remarks on Logical Form' which appeared in the Journal of the Aristotelian Society in 1929. Wittgenstein had agreed to give a talk to the Aristotelian Society that year. The Aristotelian Society insists that papers are always printed in advance, and this is why Wittgenstein's paper was published. However Wittgenstein decided shortly after the printing had taken place that the paper was worthless, and at the meeting, actually talked on another topic (see Monk, 1990, pp. 272-3 for details). After this experience, Wittgenstein became very reluctant to publish anything which he had not worked on for a long period, and this explains why he published nothing further for the next 17 years.

Now what happens under the RAE rules to academics who publish nothing? They are classified as research inactive, and their fate is not agreeable. Their research time is removed, and they have to spend more time teaching. Moreover they are at risk of being sacked. If the RAE had been in existence in 1936, and the rules had been applied without fear or favour, then this is the fate which would have overtaken Wittgenstein.

Now a defender of the RAE might at this point object to my analysis on the following grounds: 'Wittgenstein published nothing between 1930 and 1947 because he was under no pressure to do so. Had the RAE been introduced in 1936, he would certainly have "knuckled under" and published some stuff.' Unfortunately for this argument, numerous memoirs and the magnificent (1990) biography of Wittgenstein by Ray Monk have given us quite a vivid picture Wittgenstein's character, and this leaves no doubt that Wittgenstein was the last person on earth to have 'knuckled under' and obeyed the directives of the RAE.

In fact Wittgenstein, despite his great intellectual brilliance, seems to have disliked the company and habits of academics and to have preferred associating with simple folk. Karl Britton, a former student of Wittgenstein's, very clearly describes this attitude of the master (quoted from Pitcher, 1964, p. 12):

'He had, he said, only once been to high table at Trinity and the clever conversation of the dons had so horrified him that he had come out with both hands over his ears. The dons talked like that only to score: they did not even enjoy doing it. He said his own bedmaker's conversation, about the private lives of her previous gentlemen and about her own family, was far preferable: at least he could understand why she talked that way and could believe that she enjoyed it.'

As a result of these attitudes, Wittgenstein showed a strong propensity to abandon seats of academic learning, and go off to remote spots in the country where he could associate with simple country folk. This propensity manifested itself as early as 1913, where he decided to go off to live alone in a remote area of Norway for two years. Russell tried in vain to dissuade him, and wrote about it in a letter as follows (quoted from Monk, 1990, p. 91):

'I said it would be dark, & he said he hated daylight. I said it would be lonely, & he said he prostituted his mind talking to intelligent people. I said he was mad & he said God preserve him from sanity. (God certainly will.)'

This episode illustrates the extreme obstinacy and determination of Wittgenstein's character. He was really not the sort of man who would have been prepared to 'knuckle under' and obey some government regulation which he regarded as mistaken.

Wittgenstein went to Norway but did not stay for two years because of the outbreak of the First World War. After the War, despite having become famous in philosophical circles because of the publication of his *Tractatus*, he decided to give up philosophy and worked as a schoolmaster in remote Austrian villages between 1920 and 1926. He refused to attend any of the meetings of the Vienna Circle which greatly admired his work. However

Wittgenstein was eventually persuaded to return to academic life in Cambridge in 1930. Yet he remained full of longings for a simple life of manual toil in some remote country location. He even applied in 1935, at the height of Stalinism, to work as a labourer on a collective farm in Russia. Perhaps luckily for him the Russians turned down his application (see Monk, 1990, p. 351). So Wittgenstein went back to his hut in Norway for a year instead.

Many people might regard the job of being professor of philosophy at Cambridge as rather an agreeable one, but not so Wittgenstein. In a letter to Malcolm in 1945, Wittgenstein wrote: ' … the absurd job of a prof. of philosophy … is a kind of living death' (quoted from Malcolm, 1958, p. 38). At this time he was contemplating resigning his professorship at Cambridge, which he did in 1947. Just before his resignation, Wittgenstein wrote (quoted from Monk, 1990, p. 516):

'Cambridge grows more and more hateful to me. The disintegrating and putrefying English civilization. A country in which politics alternates between an evil purpose and *no* purpose.'

After resigning his chair, Wittgenstein went off in 1948 to live in a remote country district in Galway on the west coast of Ireland.

These episodes give a vivid illustration of Wittgenstein's character and tastes. In the light of these, is it possible that, if the RAE had been introduced in 1936, he would have agreed to its demands and started publishing some of his work? I find it quite inconceivable that he would have done so. Malcolm in his Memoir records (p. 49) that in the academic year 1946-7, Wittgenstein stated that 'he was not going to be "stampeded" into publishing prematurely.' In fact he had published nothing for over 17 years at that stage of his career.

If there is still any doubt on this point, it could be added that Wittgenstein was also highly contemptuous of the typical academic procedures which are enshrined in the RAE. This is illustrated vividly in letters written by Wittgenstein to Malcolm in 1945 and 1948. It should be explained that Wittgenstein was very fond of reading American detective magazines – particularly those published by Street and Smith. In the 1930s and 1940s, *Mind* was a leading English philosophy journal, as indeed it still is today. To have a series of papers published in *Mind* would be regarded as a strong point in favour of any researcher according to the usual RAE criteria. Wittgenstein, however, far from endorsing these RAE criteria is very sarcastic about them, and compares *Mind* unfavourably with the detective magazines of Street and Smith (cf. Malcolm, 1958, p. 32). In 1945 he wrote to Malcolm:

'If I read your mags I often wonder how anyone can read "Mind" with all its impotence & bankruptcy when they could read Street & Smyth mags. Well, everyone to his taste.'

In another letter to Malcolm in 1948, he elaborated the comparison:

'Your mags are wonderful. How people can read Mind if they could read Street & Smith beats me. If philosophy has anything to do with wisdom there's certainly not a grain of that in Mind, & quite often a grain in the detective stories.'

Suppose then that the RAE had been introduced in 1936. Are we seriously to suppose that Wittgenstein would have 'knuckled under' and submitted papers for publication in *Mind*? Given his character and views, it is altogether out of the question that he would have done so. His reaction is entirely predictable. In the face of such a demand, he would have undoubtedly have left Cambridge in disgust and gone off to his hut in Norway.

The effect of the introduction of the RAE in 1936 would then have been to hound Wittgenstein out of Cambridge. Hardly a result which should increase our confidence in the merits of the RAE! What actually happened was that Wittgenstein was offered a Chair in Philosophy at Cambridge in 1939, despite having published nothing for ten years. Such an appointment would of course be almost impossible under a RAE regime. Even if the members of the appointments panel were sympathetic to a candidate who had published nothing for ten years, they could hardly overlook the fact that such a professor would contribute nothing to the RAE, and would indeed set a bad example to the rest of the department. So if the RAE had been introduced in 1936, Wittgenstein would have been very unlikely to have become Professor of Philosophy at Cambridge.

Wittgenstein was perhaps rather excessively reluctant to publish, but how can we condemn his strategy in general terms? Wittgenstein was not of course really research inactive while at Cambridge. Although he published nothing between 1929 and 1951, he produced roughly thirty thousand pages of notebooks, manuscripts, and typescripts on philosophy in that period (Malcolm, 1958, p. 84). That is an average rate of about 26 pages a week. Wittgenstein's view was that he shouldn't publish anything until he had thought and rethought about it, and worked through it many times revising and correcting. He believed that only in this way could he produce philosophical work of lasting value. Now how can we say he was wrong about this? After all, his strategy worked. At the end of his long years of rethinking, revising and correcting, he produced a book (*Philosophical*

Investigations) which many regard as the philosophical masterpiece of the twentieth century.

I am not saying that every philosopher should adopt Wittgenstein's strategy. Other philosophers work in a quite different way and yet produce just as good philosophy. It is partly a matter of style and temperament. Russell, for example, who was in my opinion just as good a philosopher as Wittgenstein, worked in quite a different way. He had no inhibitions about publishing, and, when thinking about a problem, would often publish in rapid succession a series of papers considering different solutions before finally settling on a particular approach. But, although Wittgenstein's way of working is not the only one, it is certainly a possible way of working which has produced great philosophy. It is thus obviously wrong for the RAE to rule out this strategy of delaying publication, and this is a great weakness of the whole system.

Let us now consider what response a defender of the RAE might give to this objection. He or she might reply along the following lines: 'Philosophy is a peculiar intellectual discipline, and tends to attract peculiar people. Even by the standards of philosophers, Wittgenstein was exceptionally strange. Now if we turn from philosophy to more serious intellectual disciplines such as mathematics, medicine, physics or astronomy, we shall find that these scientific disciplines are carried out by less peculiar people for whom the criteria of the RAE are certainly appropriate.' To meet this challenge, I must turn to a consideration of science, and this I will do in the next chapter.

In fact we shall discover that many of the great scientific innovators had personalities which were no less unusual than Wittgenstein's. It will also emerge that Wittgenstein had some advantages which several of those who made great advances in science lacked. Wittgenstein's work was recognised very early on by individuals such as Russell and Keynes who could exercise a powerful influence in the academic world. Some other notable pioneers had the less agreeable experience of finding that their innovative work was not recognised by anyone, and indeed was rejected as absurd by those in powerful academic positions.

In considering how the RAE might affect research in science in the UK, I will apply the historical approach introduced by the case of Wittgenstein. I will consider a number of great advances in science which occurred in the past, and ask whether, if the RAE had existed in those days, it would have helped or hindered that advance. The result of these cases is the same as the result in the case of Wittgenstein – namely that the RAE, if it had been in existence, would have constituted an obstacle to the advance.

Chapter 2. Peer Reviewing and its Failures

2.1 The RAE and Peer Reviewing

The RAE relies on what is known as **peer review**. This means that the value of a researcher's work is judged by a group of researchers working in the same field – the 'peers' of the given researcher. Indeed the RAE in a sense involves a double use of peer review. To be entered for the RAE, a work usually has to be published in an academic journal, and most academic journals use peer review to assess whether submitted papers are worth publishing. Then of course the already published work is submitted to the RAE committee for a further peer review evaluation.

There is, however, a major problem with peer review. A study of history shows that it can in some cases go very wrong. It can happen that the majority of contemporary researchers in a field judge as worthless a piece of research which is later, with the benefit of historical perspective, seen as constituting a major advance. I will now consider in detail three examples of major research advances which were judged by contemporary researchers to be valueless. The first is Frege's introduction of modern mathematical logic, which has become an essential tool for computers.   The second is Semmelweis's introduction of antiseptic precautions in hospitals such as washing the hands with antiseptic.   This is now routine practice, but Semmelweis's suggestions when he made them were regarded as absurd by the contemporary medical community. The third is Copernicus' heliocentric hypothesis which, when it was introduced, was considered absurd not only by the general public but by most professional astronomers of the time. To make matters worse, what the study of history shows is that peer reviews most often go wrong for the really important research advances. Suppose a researcher makes a small, but competent, advance of a routine kind. Peer reviews in such circumstances will usually be able to give his or her work a reasonable evaluation. When, however, a researcher makes an advance which is later seen as a key innovation and a major breakthrough, peer review may very well judge it to be absurd and of no value.

I have chosen three cases which are designed to cover a range of different sciences. The first is in mathematics, the second in medicine, and the third in astronomy. I have chosen cases where a very striking scientific advance was made at a theoretical level. I do not, however, want to focus on theory and neglect practical applications. It is now generally agreed that the development of new technological applications of science is very important in order to make the UK competitive in the era of globalisation. I have therefore chosen three theoretical advances which had very important wealth-generating applications, as will be shown later.

2.2 First Case-History: Frege and Mathematical Logic

My first example is taken from the field of mathematics and I want to consider an important advance made in a branch of the subject known as mathematical logic. This advance was made by Frege in a booklet published in 1879, and which is usually referred to by its German title of *Begriffsschrift*, which means literally: 'concept-writing'. It might be objected to this example that Frege was a philosopher rather than a mathematician. It is true that Frege wrote some very important works on philosophy, but that does not make him any less a mathematician. Other famous mathematicians such as Descartes and Leibniz also wrote on philosophy. Frege worked all his life in the mathematics department of Jena university. The *Begriffsschrift* does contain some interesting philosophical remarks, but it is mainly formal in character. Its contribution is to what is now called mathematical logic, and it is difficult to deny that mathematical logic is a branch of mathematics.

Indeed Frege's *Begriffsschrift* may justly be said to have introduced modern mathematical logic. In this work Frege presents for the first time an axiomatic-deductive development of the propositional calculus and of the predicate calculus (or quantification theory). The propositional and predicate calculi are the first things introduced in any modern treatment of mathematical logic. What is still more surprising is that the expositions of these calculi in contemporary textbooks are often quite close to the original expositions of Frege. Two well-known and widely used textbooks of mathematical logic are Mendelson (1964) and Bell and Machover (1977). Mendelson introduces the propositional calculus and quantification theory in chapters 1 & 2, while Bell and Machover introduce them in chapters 1, 2 & 3. Of course they both give many results and approaches which were discovered after Frege, but they do also give an axiomatic-deductive treatment which has a lot in common with Frege's and indeed uses some of the same axioms that Frege used.[1] Frege's treatment in the *Begriffsschrift* includes what is known as higher-order logic, whereas modern treatments usually limit themselves to first-order logic. However, leaving this subtlety aside we can say that Frege's treatment of both the propositional and predicate calculi is complete from a modern point of view, though his axiomatic presentation was subsequently simplified by reducing the number of axioms. Thus Frege created in the *Begriffsschrift* a whole new formal theory which is still today taken as the core of mathematical logic.

Frege's remarkable achievement has been fully recognised by experts in the field since the 1950s. In Appendix II to his English translation of the *Begriffsschrift*, Bynum very usefully collects together some evaluations by well-known scholars writing in the 1950s and 1960s. Here are some extracts from the passages he gives. They are all quoted from Bynum, 1972, pp. 236-8.

Quine 1952 (p. 236): ' ... the logical renaissance might be identified with the publication of Frege's *Begriffsschrift* in 1879 ... 1879 did indeed usher in a renaissance, bringing quantification theory and therewith the most powerful and most characteristic instrument of modern logic ... with the aid of quantification theory modern logicians have been able to illuminate the mechanism of deduction in general, and the foundations of mathematics in particular, to a degree hitherto undreamed of.'

Dummett 1959 (p. 238): 'There can be no doubt that Boole deserves great credit for what he achieved ... however ... Boole cannot correctly be called "the father of modern logic". *The* discoveries which separate modern logic from its precursors are of course the use of quantifiers ... and a concept of a formal system, both due to Frege and neither present even in embryo in the work of Boole.'

Bochenski 1962 (p. 237): 'Among all these logicians, Gottlob Frege holds a unique place. His *Begriffsschrift* can only be compared with one other work in the whole history of logic, the *Prior Analytics* of Aristotle. The two cannot quite be put on a level, for Aristotle was the very founder of logic, while Frege could as a result only develop it. But there is a great likeness between these two gifted works.'

William and Martha Kneale 1962 (pp. 236-7): 'Frege's *Begriffsschrift* is the first really comprehensive system of formal logic. ... Frege's work ... contains all the essentials of modern logic, and it is not unfair either to his predecessors or to his successors to say that 1879 is the most important date in the history of the subject.'

Frege carried out his researches in mathematical logic for purely theoretical reasons, but, as so often happens, his results turned out to be of great practical importance. Mathematical logic is one of the fundamental tools of present-day computer science, and one can further say that the computer as we know it today could not have developed without a prior development of mathematical logic. Detailed accounts of the use of mathematical logic in computer science and in the development of computing are contained in Davis (1988a & b) and in Gillies (2002). There are many specific examples of the application of mathematical logic in computer science, but at a very fundamental level one can say that the *Begriffsschrift* is the first example of a fully formalised language, and so, in a sense, the precursor of all programming languages (see Davis, 1988b, p. 316).

Thus Frege's research turned out to provide some of the fundamental tools for a wealth-generating technological advance. Consequently Frege's research work must be the kind of research work which a nation like the UK should try to encourage. This brings us to the question of whether Frege's research would have been helped if there had been a RAE regime operating in Germany in his day. Suppose there had been a German RAE in the 1880s, how would Frege have performed? The answer is: 'not very well.'

In Appendix I to his translation of the *Begriffsschrift*, Bynum gives in full the contemporary reviews of the work, all written in the years 1879 and 1880. It is very interesting to compare these with the evaluations of the same work made with the benefit of historical perspective in the 1950s and the 1960s. These are given by Bynum in his Appendix II, and we have already quoted some passages.

Turning now to the contemporary reviews of the *Begriffsschrift*, they were 6 in number – all quotations from them will be from the versions in Bynum, 1972, pp. 209-35. 4 were written by Germans, 1 by a Frenchman (Tannery) and 1 by an Englishman (Venn). Only one of these reviews, which was written by a German, Lasswitz, is favourable. The other 3 German reviews do make some favourable remarks, but one cannot help wondering whether these are designed to be polite to a compatriot and colleague, since they are contradicted by the majority of the detailed comments on the work which are highly unfavourable. Thus Hoppe concludes his review by saying (p. 210): 'On the whole, the book, as suggestive and pioneering, is worth while.' However earlier in the same review he had written (p. 209): '... we doubt that anything has been gained by the invented formula language itself.' Similarly Michaelis concludes his review (p. 218): 'His work ... certainly does not lack importance.' However, this rather contradicts the following harsh judgement given in the body of the review, where Michaelis says (p. 217): ' ... Frege has to pass over many things in formal logic and detract even more from its content. ... The content of logic which has been much too meagre up to now, should not be decreased, but increased.' In contrast to the later critics who saw Frege as having made an enormous step forward in logic, Michaelis actually thinks that Frege has decreased, or detracted from, the content of logic. However, the harshest German review comes from the most famous German logician of the time: Schröder. Schröder actually upbraids Lasswitz for having written a review supporting the *Begriffsschrift*, and says of this review (p. 220) that he casts 'a disapproving glance at it'. He refers to Lasswitz later (p. 221) as 'the Jena reviewer', which seems to imply that Lasswitz's favourable judgement arises from some personal connection with

Frege. Schröder's own judgement on the *Begriffsschrift* is very negative indeed. He thinks that Frege has done nothing which has not already been done much better by other people. As he says (p. 220): ' ... the present little book makes an advance which I should consider very creditable, if a large part of what it attempts had not already been accomplished by someone else, and indeed (as I shall prove) in a doubtlessly more adequate fashion.' It soon becomes clear that this other person is Boole. Indeed Schröder goes on to say (p. 221) that, leaving aside the question of function and generality and some applications, ' ... the book is devoted to the establishment of a formula language, which essentially coincides with Boole's mode of presenting *judgements* and Boole's calculus of judgments, and which certainly in no way achieves more.' Here Schröder does seem to make an exception in favour of Frege's treatment of generality but this appearance is deceptive for he later goes on to say that Frege's treatment of generality is in no way superior to the Boolean. He writes (pp. 229-30): 'Now in the section concerning "generality", Frege correctly lays down stipulations that permit him to express such judgements precisely. I shall not follow him slavishly here; but on the contrary, show that one may not perchance find a justification here for his other deviations from Boole's notation, and the analogous modification or extension can easily be achieved in Boolean notation as well.' (Logicians will at once see from this that Schröder has completely failed to grasp the importance of introducing the quantifiers.) But could Frege at least be defended on the grounds that he has shed some light on the logical nature of *arithmetical* judgements? 'Not so', argues Schröder, 'for that matter too has already been cleared up by someone else.' In his own words (p. 231): 'According to the author, he undertook the entire work with the intention of obtaining complete clarity with regard to the logical nature of *arithmetical* judgements, and above all to test "how far one could get in arithmetic by means of logical deductions alone". If I have properly understood what the author wishes to do, then this point would also be, in large measure, already settled – namely, through the perceptive investigations of Hermann Grassmann.' After dismissing Frege's work so completely, it is rather surprising that Schröder concludes (p. 231): 'May my comments, however, have the over-all effect of encouraging the author to further his research, rather than discouraging him.' Perhaps Schröder felt some pangs of guilt about writing so harshly about the work of a young researcher in his field. The two non-German reviews of the *Begriffsschrift* are if anything even more dismissive than the German reviews, and contain no favourable remarks at all. Tannery in France writes (p. 233): 'In such circumstances, we should have a right to demand complete clarity or a great simplification of formulas or important results. But much to the contrary, the explanations are insufficient, the notations are excessively complex; and as far as applications are concerned, they remain only promises.' Nowadays one of Frege's great advances is considered to be the replacement of the Aristotelian analysis in terms of subject and predicate by an analysis using function and argument. Tannery notes this change but regards it as a mistake (p. 233): 'The [author] abolishes the concepts of *subject* and *predicate* and replaces them by others which he calls *function* and *argument*. ... We cannot deny that this conception does not seem to be very fruitful.' Finally Venn in England entirely agrees with Schröder that Frege has made no advance over Boole and has indeed taken a step backwards. Venn writes (p. 234): ' ... it does not seem to me that Dr. Frege's scheme can for a moment compare with that of Boole. I should suppose, from his making no reference whatever to the latter, that he has not seen it, nor any of the modifications of it with which we are familiar here. Certainly the merits which he claims as novel for his own method are common to every symbolic method.' Venn, moreover, has no kind words at the end of his review, but concludes by saying (p. 235): ' ... Dr Frege's system ... seems to me cumbrous and inconvenient.' It is worth noting here that Frege's advances over Boole which seem so obvious today and which are mentioned by Dummett in the passage quoted above, were not appreciated at all by Schröder and Venn – two of the leading logicians of Frege's time. So to sum up. If we go carefully through the six contemporary reviews of Frege's *Begriffsschrift*, we find only one which takes a positive view of Frege's work. In the other five, there is a consensus to be found that the *Begriffsschrift* makes no advance on what has already been done, particularly by Boole and the Booleans, and indeed that it is in many respects inferior to and a step back from already existing logical works.

What is remarkable is that Frege was not discouraged by these damning reviews, but continued his work on his logicist programme for the next 24 years. However, his subsequent books were, if anything, even less successful than the *Begriffsschrift*. The *Foundations of Arithmetic* published in 1884 received only 3 reviews – all unfavourable. In 1891 Frege wanted to publish a third book in the series, but, perhaps not surprisingly, found it hard to find a publisher. Eventually, however, (Bynum, 1972, p. 34): 'the publisher Hermann Pohle in Jena ... agreed to print the book in two instalments, the publication of the second part to be dependent upon a good reception of the first. So, in late 1893, the first volume of *The Basic Laws of Arithmetic* appeared.' This book got only two reviews – both unfavourable. In the light of this Frege had to publish the second volume which appeared in 1903, at his own expense. In the 1890s and 1900s a few avant-garde researchers – notably Peano and Russell – did begin to study and develop Frege's ideas. However, even when Frege retired from Jena at the age of 70 in 1918, general recognition had still eluded him. The situation was well summed-up by Bochenski in 1962 (quoted from Bynum, 1972, pp. 237-8):

'It is a remarkable fact that this logician of them all had to wait twenty years before he was at all noticed, and another twenty before his full strictness

18

of procedure was resumed by Lukasiewicz. In this last respect, everything published between 1879 and 1921 fell below the standard of Frege, and it is seldom attained even today.'

Anyone who is concerned with formulating policies concerned with research, should in my opinion read carefully the two appendices to Bynum, 1972. They amount to only 30 pages, but they demonstrate in a conclusive fashion that the method of peer review can, in some cases, go very wrong. It does happen that the majority of contemporary researchers in a field can judge as worthless a piece of research which is later, with the benefit of historical perspective, seen as constituting a major advance.

Now the RAE does clearly rely on peer review because the value of each researcher is judged by a committee of experts in the field. Indeed, as we have remarked, the RAE in a sense involves a double use of peer review, because the members of the RAE consider only research which has been published, and, to get a piece of work published, a researcher has usually to submit it to a journal which uses peer review to assess whether it is worth publishing. The problem facing those like Frege, whose work is judged of little value by the majority of their peers, is that they may find it difficult to publish at all. This applied to Frege himself. He wrote two papers replying to the criticism of Schröder and Venn that his work was inferior to that of Boole. However he was unable to publish these papers (cf. Bynum, 1972, p. 21), and they only appeared long after Frege's death. Those researchers who find their peers against their work will certainly be excluded from publishing in the more famous journals and may have to resort to publishing in lower rated journals or even to publishing the material in book form at their own expense, as Frege did in 1903. Now theoretically the RAE committee reads carefully and judges on their merits all the works submitted to it, but of course in practice papers which have appeared in high ranking journals, or books which have been published by prestigious firms such as Oxford University Press, are likely to be judged more favourably. Conversely papers which have appeared in low ranking journals, or, worse still, books published at the author's own expense – something usually called 'vanity publishing' – are likely to be judged more harshly. We have therefore to conclude that if the RAE had existed in Germany in the 1880s Frege would have got a very low rating.

Even in the RAE free Germany of the period, Frege did not have an easy time. A fascinating portrait of him in the years 1910-14 is given by Carnap in his intellectual autobiography (Carnap, 1963). Carnap's involvement with Frege appears to have come about rather by chance. Carnap's family lived in Jena, and Carnap went to the local university where Frege taught. Carnap writes (1963, p. 5):
'In the fall of 1910, I attended Frege's course "Begriffsschrift"

(conceptual notation, ideography), out of curiosity, not knowing anything either of the man or the subject except for a friend's remark that somebody had found it interesting. We found a very small number of other students, there. Frege looked old beyond his years. He was of small stature, rather shy, extremely introverted. He seldom looked at the audience. Ordinarily we saw only his back, while he drew the strange diagrams of his symbolism on the blackboard and explained them. Never did a student ask a question or make a remark, whether during the lecture or afterwards. The possibility of a discussion seemed to be out of the question.'

Earlier in his account, Carnap says (1963, p. 4):

'Gottlob Frege (1848-1925) was at that time, although past 60, only Professor Extraordinarius (Associate Professor) of mathematics in Jena. His work was practically unknown in Germany; neither mathematicians nor philosophers paid any attention to it. It was obvious that Frege was deeply disappointed and sometimes bitter about this dead silence.'

Carnap, however, took a liking to Frege's work and attended his two advanced courses "Begriffsschrift II" in 1913 and his course Logik in der Mathematik in 1914. Carnap records that "Begriffsschrift II" was attended by 3 students: Carnap, a friend of Carnap's, and (Carnap, 1963, p. 5) 'a retired major of the army who studied some of the new ideas in mathematics as a hobby.'

We can see from this that Frege's career was hardly a great success, but, if there had been a RAE regime in Germany, things would have gone even worse for him. As we have seen, Frege would undoubtedly have got a low rating in the RAE exercise, and the inevitable penalties would have fallen on his head. His research time would have been cut and he would have been forced to take on extra teaching duties. Thus he would not have had the necessary research time to develop his mathematical logic. Moreover, as we can see from Carnap's description, Frege may not have performed particularly well as a teacher. He seemed to attract very few students, and his teaching technique does not appear to have been of the kind recommended by educational experts. Having failed as both a researcher and a teacher, there is little doubt than, under a RAE regime, Frege would have been forced to retire early rather than allowed to stay on until he was 70. Thus Carnap would never have been able to attend his lectures, and the development and diffusion of the new important ideas of mathematical logic would have been held up still further.

2.3 Second Case-History: Semmelweis and Antisepsis

My second case-history, as we shall see, has many points in common with the first. However, it does differ very strikingly as regards the branch of science in which the research was conducted. Frege's research was purely theoretical, and was carried out in a branch of mathematics, mathematical logic, which is closely linked to philosophy. Semmelweis's research by contrast was highly empirical, and was carried out in medicine. In fact Semmelweis's investigation was into the causes of a terrible disease (puerperal fever) which affected women who had just given birth. Puerperal fever was, at the time, the principal cause of death in childbirth.

Semmelweis was Hungarian, but studied medicine at the University of Vienna. In 1844 he qualified as a doctor, and, later in the same year obtained the degree of Master of Midwifery. From then until 1849, he held the posts of either aspirant to assistant or full assistant at the first maternity clinic in Vienna. It was during this period that he carried out his research.[2]

The Vienna Maternity Hospital was divided into two clinics from 1833. Patients were admitted to the two clinics on alternate days thereby producing, unintentionally, a system of random allocation. Between 1833 and 1840, medical students, doctors and midwives attended both clinics, but, thereafter, although doctors went to both clinics, the first clinic only was used for the instruction of medical students who were all male in those days, and the second clinic was reserved for the instruction of midwives. When Semmelweis began working as a full assistant in 1846, the mortality statistics showed a strange phenomenon

Between 1833 and 1840, the death rates in the two clinics had been comparable, but, in the period 1841-46, the death rate in the first clinic was 9.92% and in the second clinic 3.88%. The first figure is more than 2.5 times the second – a difference which is certainly statistically significant. The quoted figures actually underestimate the difference since some severe cases of puerperal fever were removed from the first clinic to the general hospital where they died – thereby disappearing from the first clinic's mortality statistics. This rarely happened in the second clinic. Semmelweis was puzzled and set himself the task of finding the cause of the higher death rate in the first clinic.

Semmelweis followed a procedure rather similar to Popper's conjectures and refutations. He considered in turn a number of hypotheses as to what might be the cause of the difference between the two clinics. He then compared these hypotheses to the facts, and found that each one of a long series of hypotheses was refuted by this comparison. Eventually, however,

Semmelweis did hit on a hypothesis which was corroborated by the observations.

The first hypothesis considered by Semmelweis was that the higher death rate in the first clinic was due to 'atmospheric-cosmic-terrestial' factors. This sounds strange but is just a way of referring to the miasma theory of disease which was standard at the time. However Semmelweis pointed out that it could not explain the different mortality rates in the first and second clinics. These were under the same roof and had an ante-room in common. So they must be exposed to the same 'atmospheric-cosmic-terrestial' influences. Yet the death rates in the two clinics were very different.

The next hypothesis was that overcrowding was the key factor, but this too was easily refuted since the second clinic was always more crowded than the first, which, not surprisingly had acquired an evil reputation among the patients, almost all of whom tried to avoid it.

In this sort of way Semmelweis eliminated quite a number of curious hypotheses. One concerned the appearance of a priest to give the last sacrament to a dying woman. The arrangement of the rooms meant that the priest, arrayed in his robes, and with an attendant before him ringing a bell had to pass through five wards of the first clinic before reaching the sickroom where the woman lay dying. The priest had, however, direct access to the sickroom in the case of the second clinic. The hypothesis then was that the terrifying psychological effect of the priest's appearance debilitated patients in the first clinic, and made them more liable to puerperal fever. Semmelweis persuaded the priest to come by a less direct route, without bells, and without passing through the other clinic rooms. The two clinics were made identical in this respect as well, but the mortality rate was unaffected.

After trying out these hypotheses and others unsuccessfully, Semmelweis was in a depressed state in the winter of 1846-7. However a tragic event early in 1847 led him to formulate a new hypothesis. On 20th March 1847, Semmelweis heard with sorrow of the death of Professor Kolletschka. In the course of a post-mortem examination, Professor Kolletschka had received a wound on his finger from the knife of one of the students helping to carry out the autopsy. As a result Kolletschka died not long afterwards of a disease very similar to puerperal fever. Semmelweis reasoned that Kolletschka's death had been owing to cadaverous matter entering his bloodstream. Could the same cause explain the higher death rate of patients in the first clinic? In fact professors, assistants and students often went directly from dissecting corpses to examining patients in the first clinic. It is true that they washed their hands with soap and water, but perhaps some cadaverous particles still adhered to their hands. Indeed this seemed probable since their hands often retained a cadaverous odour after washing. The doctors and medical students might then infect some of the patients in the first clinic with these cadaverous particles, thereby giving them puerperal fever. This would explain why the death rate was lower in the second clinic, since the student midwives did not carry out post-mortems.

In order to test this hypothesis, Semmelweis, from some time in May 1847, required everyone to wash their hands in disinfectant before making examinations. At first he used *chlorina liquida*, but, as this was rather expensive, chlorinated lime was substituted. The result was dramatic. In 1848 the mortality rate in the first clinic fell to 1.27%, while that in the second clinic was 1.30%. This was the first time the mortality rate in the first clinic had been lower than that of the second clinic since the medical students had been divided from the student midwives in 1841.

Through a consideration of some further cases, Semmelweis extended his theory to the view that, not just cadaverous particles, but any decaying organic matter, could cause puerperal fever if it entered the bloodstream of a patient.

Let us now look at Semmelweis's theory from a modern point of view. Puerperal fever is now known as 'post-partum sepsis' and is considered to be a bacterial infection. The bacterium principally responsible is *streptococcus pyogenes*, but other *streptococci* and *staphylococci* may be involved. Thus, from a modern point of view, cadaverous particles and other decaying organic matter would not necessarily cause puerperal fever but only if they contain a large enough quantity of living *streptococci* and *staphylococci*. However as putrid matter derived from living organisms is a good source of such bacteria, Semmelweis was not far wrong.

As for the hand washing recommended by Semmelweis, that is of course absolutely standard in hospitals. Medical staff have to wash their hands in antiseptic soap (hibiscrub), and there is also a gelatinous substance (alcogel) which is squirted on to the hand. Naturally a doctor's hands must be sterilised in this way before examining any patient – exactly as Semmelweis recommended. Recently new regulations have been introduced in hospitals in the UK requiring visitors also to wash their hands in disinfectant.

Not only are Semmelweis's views regarded as largely correct form a modern point of view, but the investigation which led him to them is now held up as model of good scientific method.   In fact Hempel in his 1966 book: *Philosophy of Natural Science* gives a number of examples of what he regards as excellent scientific investigations, and the very first of these is Semmelweis's research into puerperal fever.

This then is the modern point of view, but how did Semmelweis's contemporaries react to his new theory of the cause of puerperal fever and the practical recommendations based on it? The short answer is that Semmelweis's reception by his contemporaries was almost exactly the same as Frege's. Semmelweis did manage to persuade one or two doctors of the truth of his findings, but the vast majority of the medical profession rejected his theory and ignored the practical recommendations based upon it. I discuss some of the detailed responses to Semmelweis in my longer account of the subject (see Gillies, 2005, pp. 178-9). Here I will only mention one typical reaction. After Semmelweis had made his discovery in 1848, he and some of his friends in Vienna wrote about them to the directors of several maternity hospitals. Simpson of Edinburgh replied somewhat rudely to this letter saying that its authors obviously had not studied the obstetrical literature in English. Simpson was of course a very important figure in the medical world of the time. He had introduced the use of chloroform for operations, and had recommended its use as a pain-killer in childbirth. His response to Semmelweis and his friends is very similar in character to Venn's review of Frege's *Begriffsschrift*.

In Vienna the Professor and Head of the Maternity Clinics, Johann Klein, was opposed to Semmelweis's ideas, and his opposition, and that of others, caused Semmelweis to leave Vienna in 1850. He did however get a position in a Maternity Hospital at Budapest in his native Hungary. Here he wrote up his new theory of the causes of puerperal fever, and answered the objections which had been made to it. These writings were published in book form in 1861, but once again had no success in persuading the medical profession to adopt his ideas.

Semmelweis's case is very similar to Frege's. Semmelweis, like Frege, had great difficulties, and, if there had been a RAE regime at the time, these difficulties would have become worse. Semmelweis's work would obviously have been judged by peer review to have no value, and his allowance of research time would have been reduced, so that he might not have had the time to write up his results in book form and to answer his critics.

The failure of the research community to recognise Semmelweis's work had of course much more serious consequences than the corresponding failure to appreciate Frege's innovations. In the twenty years after 1847 when Semmelweis made his basic discoveries, hospitals throughout the world were plagued with what were known as 'hospital diseases', that is to say, diseases which a patient entering a hospital was very likely to contract. These included not just puerperal fever, but a whole range of other unpleasant illnesses. There were wound sepsis, hospital gangrene, tetanus, and spreading gangrene, erysipelas (or 'St. Anthony's fire'), pyaemia and septicaemia which are two different forms of blood poisoning, and so on. Many of these diseases were fatal. From the modern point of view, they are all bacterial diseases which can be conquered by applying the kind of antiseptic precautions recommended by Semmelweis.

In 1871, over twenty years after his rather abrupt reply to Semmelweis and his friends, Simpson of Edinburgh wrote a series of articles on 'Hospitalism'. These contained his famous claim, well-supported by statistics, that 'the man laid on the operating-table in one of our surgical hospitals is exposed to more chances of death than the English soldier on the field of Waterloo'. Simpson thought that hospitals infected with pyaemia might have to be demolished completely. So serious was the crisis, that he even recommended replacing hospitals by villages of small iron huts to accommodate one or two patients, which were to be pulled down and re-erected periodically. Luckily the theory and practice of antisepsis were introduced in Britain by Lister in 1865, and were supported by the germ theory of disease developed by Pasteur in France and Koch in Germany. The new antiseptic methods had become general by the mid 1880s, so that the hospital crisis was averted. All the same, the failure to recognise Semmelweis's work must have cost the lives of many patients.

In my longer paper on the Semmelweis case (Gillies, 2005, pp. 180-1), I argue that, in the history and philosophy of science, it is customary to cite historical examples of excellent science in order to exemplify what are claimed to be good methodological principles for science. However instances in which the scientific community makes a mistake, as happened in the Semmelweis case or that of Frege, can also be valuable in suggesting new rules of practice designed to make such mistakes less likely in the future. From this point of view, the RAE is clearly a step backwards. Instead of learning from the mistakes which were made regarding Frege and Semmelweis, and introducing a system designed to make such mistakes less likely in the future, it does the opposite. If the RAE had been in existence in the days of Frege and Semmelweis, it would, as we have seen, have made their position even worse than it already was. Naturally the same will apply to any future brilliant innovators like Frege and Semmelweis who have the misfortune to be working in a RAE regime.

2.4 Third Case-History: Copernicus and Astronomy

I now turn to my third example which I will deal with more concisely both because it is more familiar and because my general line of argument should by now have become fairly clear. However, it is worth looking at this example because it deals with yet another branch of science (astronomy) and also a different historical period.[3]

Copernicus (1473-1543) was born in what is now Poland and studied at Universities in both Poland and Italy. Through the influence of his uncle, he obtained the post of Canon of Frauenberg Cathedral in 1497, and held this position until his death. Copernicus' duties as canon left him plenty of time for other activities, and he seems to have devoted much of this time to developing in detail his new theory of the universe. This was published as *De Revolutionibus Orbium Caelestium*, when Copernicus was on his death bed. In the preface Copernicus states that he had meditated on this work for more than 36 years.

There is little doubt that during Copernicus' lifetime and for more than 50 or 60 years after his death, his view that the Earth moved was regarded as absurd, not only by the vast majority of the general public, but also by the vast majority of those who were expert in astronomy. It is significant that *De Revolutionibus* was not put on the index by the Roman Catholic Church until 1616. It was not until then that Copernicanism had sufficient adherents to be considered a threat.

Although the majority of expert astronomers of the period would have dismissed the Copernican view as absurd, a few such astronomers, notably Kepler and Galileo, did side with Copernicus and carried out researches developing his theory until, in due course, it won general acceptance by astronomers not influenced by the Roman Catholic Church's opposition.

Copernicus' research, like that of Frege and Semmelweis, had very important practical applications. Despite the Roman Catholic Church's opposition to his theory, his calculations were used in the reform of the calendar carried out by Pope Gregory XIII in 1582. Ironically the Protestant countries, whose astronomers were the first to accept the Copernican theory, rejected the Gregorian calendar for a long time on the grounds that it had been introduced by the Roman Catholic Church and must presumably therefore be bad. Copernicus' theory was also used to produce improved astronomical tables. Reinhold used *De Revolutionibus* in the production of his Prutenic Tables which appeared in 1551. These were the first complete tables prepared in Europe for three centuries. In 1627, they were superseded by the Rudolfine Tables which Kepler produced using his much improved version of Copernicus' theory. The Rudolfine Tables were clearly superior to all astronomical tables in use before. Of course astronomical tables were applied in navigation, and so were an important tool for promoting the growth of European maritime trade.

Let us now once again consider how Copernicus would have been affected if, instead of being a Canon of Frauenberg, he had lived under a RAE regime. Of course it is indeed rather anachronistic to suppose that something like the

RAE might have been in existence in such a distant historical period. Yet I think we can still say with confidence that if it had existed then, it would have impacted negatively on Copernicus. Under a RAE regime, Copernicus would not have been allowed to continue his research peacefully as a Canon of Frauenberg. On the contrary, he would have been brought to account to make sure he was not wasting the tax-payers' money. In order to be allowed time to continue his research, he would have had to submit samples of his research work to a committee of experts in the field. Now nearly all these experts, as we have already pointed out, would have judged that Copernicus's research was absurd and not worth funding. Thus Copernicus would have been sent off to a teaching university with little time for research, and would have had to devote most of his time to teaching astronomy to undergraduates. Naturally, as the syllabus would have been determined by the majority of his colleagues, he would have had to teach, not his new theory, but the standard Aristotelian-Ptolemaic account of astronomy. So Copernicus, under a system of funding of RAE type, would have been deprived of his research time, and forced to spend his days teaching the Aristotelian-Ptolemaic account of astronomy. Meanwhile the leading experts of the Aristotelian-Ptolemaic theory would have had posts at the well-funded research universities giving them plenty of time to pursue their research. No doubt they would have developed Aristotelian-Ptolemaic theory by means of ever more mathematically ingenious combinations of epicycles. It need hardly be said that all this would have acted as an extreme dampener on the progress of astronomy.

I have given three examples of cases in which a regime of RAE type would have impeded rather than helped scientific advance. Of course many more cases along the same lines could be described, but it will now be more fruitful to turn from history of science to philosophy of science. In the next chapter, I will try to analyse the factors, which in the cases of Copernicus, Frege and Semmelweis, led to the failure of the peer review method. As we shall see, this is not a problem which has arisen in just a few cases, but is an underlying pattern in the development of science.

Chapter 3. Explanation of the Failure of Peer Reviewing. Paradigms and Research Programmes

But how is it possible for peer reviews to go so wrong, and to judge as worthless what are later seen as major advances in the subject? At first it may seem paradoxical that this should occur. After all, the peers, who do the reviewing, are all experts in the field and active researchers. Surely they, of all people, should be able to recognise good research when they see it. Despite the apparent strangeness of this situation, the reasons why it occurs can in fact be quite well explained using ideas from the philosophy of science, more specifically using Kuhn's paradigms, and Lakatos' research programmes.

3.1 Paradigms

Kuhn's theory of scientific development is set out in his *The Structure of Scientific Revolutions* (1962). Kuhn's view is that science develops through periods of *normal science* which are characterised by the dominance of a *paradigm*, but which are interrupted by occasional revolutions during which the old paradigm is replaced by a new one. I will illustrate this theory by considering in turn the three scientific revolutions which constitute Kuhn's main examples. These are (i) the Copernican Revolution, (ii) the Chemical Revolution, and (iii) the Einsteinian Revolution.

(i) *The Copernican Revolution.* Kuhn's first book, published in 1957 was entitled: The Copernican Revolution, and it was probably this example more than any other which led him to his general model of scientific revolutions. From late Greek times until Copernicus, astronomy was dominated by the Aristotelian-Ptolemaic paradigm. The earth was considered to be stationary at the centre of the universe. The different movements of sublunary and heavenly bodies were described by Aristotelian mechanics. The astronomer had to describe and predict the movements of the Sun, Moon and planets as accurately as possible, using the Ptolemaic scheme of epicycles, and other geometrical devices. This was the normal science of the time.

Copernicus, however, challenged the dominant paradigm by suggesting that the Earth spun on its axis and moved round the Sun. He worked out this alternative theory in as detailed a mathematical fashion as Ptolemy's. His results were published in his book *De Revolutionibus Orbium Caelestium* in 1543, and this publication inaugurated a revolutionary period during which the old Aristotelian-Ptolemaic paradigm was overthrown and replaced by a new paradigm – first formulated in detail by Newton in *Philosophiae*

Naturalis Principia Mathematica (1687).

(ii) *The Chemical Revolution*. The main theme of the chemical revolution was the replacement of the *phlogiston* theory by the *oxygen* theory, though there were many other important changes as well. According to the phlogiston theory, bodies are inflammable if they contain a substance called phlogiston, and this is released when the body burns. The phlogiston theory was also used to explain the calcination of metals. When a metal is heated in air, in many cases it turns into a powder known as the *calx*, e.g. iron → rust. Conversely the calx is usually found in ores of the metal, and the metal itself could often be obtained by heating with charcoal. These transformations were explained by postulating that

$$\text{calx} + \text{phlogiston} = \text{metal}$$

When we heat a metal, phlogiston is given off, and the calx remains. Conversely when we heat the calx with charcoal, since charcoal is very rich in phlogiston because it burns easily, the phlogiston from the charcoal combines with the calx to give the metal.

In the oxygen theory, burning is explained as the combination of the substance with oxygen; while the calx is identified with the oxide of the metal. So turning a metal into its calx by heating in air is explained by the equation

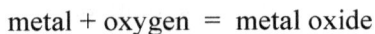

$$\text{metal} + \text{oxygen} = \text{metal oxide}$$

Similarly obtaining the metal by heating the calx with charcoal is explained by the equation

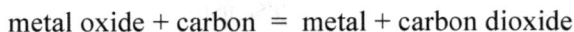

$$\text{metal oxide} + \text{carbon} = \text{metal} + \text{carbon dioxide}$$

The oxygen theory was developed by Lavoisier. At the beginning of his researches in 1772, he was already sceptical of the then dominant phlogiston theory. In the next decade or so, many experimental discoveries concerning gases were made. These discoveries were mainly owing to the English experimental chemists – particularly Priestley and Cavendish. However, these English chemists remained faithful to the phlogiston theory. For example Priestley referred to what we now call oxygen as dephlogisticated air. Lavoisier, on the other hand, reinterpreted their results in terms of his new and developing oxygen theory. Lavoisier's new paradigm for chemistry was set out in his *Traité élémentaire de chimie* of 1789, and within a few years it was adopted by the majority of chemists. Priestley, however, who lived until 1804, never gave up the phlogiston theory.

(iii) *The Einsteinian Revolution.* The triumph of the Newtonian paradigm initiated a new period of normal science for astronomy (c. 1700–1900). The dominant paradigm consisted of Newtonian mechanics including the law of gravity, and the normal scientist had to use this tool to explain the motions of the heavenly bodies in detail – comets, perturbations of the planets and the moon, etc. In the Einsteinian revolution (c.1900–1920), however, the Newtonian paradigm was replaced by the special and general theories of relativity.

Further research in the philosophy of science has shown that Kuhn's model, with some modifications, can be extended to mathematics and medicine. Thus Frege's work can be considered as a initiating a revolution in logic analogous to the Copernican revolution in astronomy. The change was from an Aristotelian paradigm, whose core was the theory of the syllogism, to a new paradigm whose core was propositional and first-order predicate calculus.[4] Then again Semmelweis's investigation can be seen as one of the first steps in a revolution in medicine. The change was from a paradigm whose core was the miasma and contagion theories of disease to a new paradigm with the germ theory of disease as its core.[5]

Now one of the strengths of Kuhn's theory is that it explains why the scientific community made such mistaken judgements regarding figures like Copernicus, Semmelweis and Frege. On Kuhn's model, at the beginning of a revolution almost all the researchers in the field accept the dominant paradigm, and, from the point of view of this paradigm, the new revolutionary approach will indeed seem absurd.

Another important consequence of Kuhn's theory is that the mistaken judgements regarding Copernicus, Semmelweis and Frege are not features of science's past, but are likely to recur over and over again. Of course, long before Kuhn, the Copernican revolution had been studied by historians of science. However, it tended to be regarded as something of a 'one-off' event – a dramatic change which had introduced modern science, but was not likely to recur. This is reflected in the fact that it was often referred to as: *The* Scientific Revolution. Kuhn's originality was to suggest that all branches of science develop through periodic revolutions. This new view was obviously suggested by the revolution in physics in the first few decades of the twentieth century which led to the triumph of relativity theory and quantum mechanics. Kuhn's model of scientific development was roughly as follows. For most of the time we have 'normal science' in which the scientists working in a particular area all, except perhaps for a few dissidents, accept the same dominant paradigm.   Within the framework of that paradigm, steady, if perhaps somewhat slow, progress is made. Every so often, however, a period of revolution occurs in which the previously dominant paradigm comes to be criticized by a small number of revolutionary scientists. This small group succeeds in developing a new paradigm, and in persuading their colleagues to accept it. Thus there comes about a revolutionary shift from the old paradigm to a new one. Although revolutions occur only occasionally in the development of a field of science, such revolutions are the exciting times in which really big progress is made in the field.

Kuhn's model of scientific development is, in my view, strongly confirmed by studies in the history of science. Indeed it applies not just to the natural sciences considered by Kuhn, but also to science in the broader sense considered in this book which includes also mathematics and medicine. Kuhn's model has the great merit that it explains the historical failures of peer review. Such failures occur when a new approach introducing a new paradigm is introduced. To the peer reviewers who have all been trained in the old paradigm and accept it implicitly, this new approach which contradicts the old paradigm appears absurd. Later, when the new paradigm has become accepted, and the old paradigm largely forgotten, it is the objections of the peer reviewers which seem absurd and inexplicable. How could such intelligent researchers have failed to appreciate what to us is so obviously a major advance? The answer is that the work appears to us to be a major advance because we have been trained in - and implicitly accept - the new paradigm, while to the original peer reviewers it appeared to be absurd because they had been trained in - and implicitly accepted - the old paradigm.

3.2 Research Programmes

However, the failure of peer review need not be exclusively associated with scientific revolutions, and paradigm shifts. It can occur in what Kuhn calls 'normal science' as well. To see this, let us suppose that research is being carried out on some problem and that four different research programmes have been proposed to solve it. We can further suppose that all four of the programmes are compatible with the dominant paradigm, so that we are not dealing with revolutionary science. It may be almost impossible to say at the beginning which of the four programmes is going to lead to success. Suppose it turns out to be programme number 3. Let us suppose further (which indeed is often the case) that initially programme 3 attracts many fewer researchers than programmes 1, 2 & 4. Now it is characteristic of most researchers that they think their own approach to the problem is the correct one, and that other approaches are misguided. If a peer review is conducted by a committee whose researchers are a random sample of those working on the problem, then the majority will be working on programmes 1, 2 & 4, and are therefore very likely to give a negative judgement on programme 3. As the result of the recommendation of such a peer review, funding might be withdrawn from programme 3, and the solution of the problem might remain undiscovered for a long time.

An important principle emerges from this, namely that research assessment systems which, like the RAE, are based on peer review, are likely to concentrate funding on the most popular, or mainstream, research programmes, while withdrawing funding from, and sometimes closing down altogether, minority research programmes on which few researchers are working. Actually the Kuhnian examples of revolutionary science and paradigm shifts are only a special case of this principle. In a scientific revolution, the scientists who introduce a new research programme based on a new paradigm, or who are among the first to start working on it, will almost certainly be a minority within the research community of the time. This tends to be obscured in histories of science since these pioneering scientists are the ones who are remembered and whose works are studied, while the majority who still accepted the old paradigm are forgotten. Thus, in the Copernican revolution, we remember Galileo and Kepler because they accepted the Copernican view, and consequently make striking advances. Their contemporaries who continued working in the old Aristotelian-Ptolemaic paradigm are largely forgotten, even though they were the majority at the time.

Now sometimes the mainstream research programme cracks the problems being tackled. Sometimes, however, it is a very minority research programme only adopted by a few researchers which leads to the major advances. A recent example of this is the discovery that a form of cervical cancer is caused by a preceding infection by the papilloma virus. In 2008 zur Hausen was awarded the Nobel prize for this discovery. In the research which led to the discovery, however, the majority of researchers favoured the view that the causal agent for cervical cancer was a herpes virus and not a papilloma virus. zur Hausen was one of the few who favoured the papilloma virus.

Examples like this show that cutting off funding from minority research programmes is likely to be very harmful to the progress of science. Yet a system such as the RAE which is based on peer reviewing is likely to have just such an effect. This point leads on to a distinction between two types of error which can be made in research funding, and this is something which will be considered in the next chapter.

Chapter 4. Type 1 and Type 2 Errors. Throwing away the Pink Diamonds

4.1 Type 1 and Type 2 Errors

I will next make a distinction which is analogous to one made in the theory of statistical tests. Statistical tests are said to be liable to two types of error (Type 1 error, and Type 2 error). A Type 1 error occurs if the test leads to the rejection of a hypothesis which is in fact true. A Type 2 error occurs if the test leads to the confirmation of a hypothesis which is in fact false. Analogously we could say that a research assessment procedure commits a Type 1 error if it leads to funding being withdrawn from a researcher or research programme which would have obtained excellent results had it been continued. A research assessment procedure commits a Type 2 error if it leads to funding being continued for a researcher or research programme which obtains no good results however long it goes on. This distinction leads to the following general criticism of the RAE. The RAE concentrates exclusively on eliminating Type 2 errors. The idea behind the RAE is to make research more cost effective by withdrawing funds from bad researchers and giving them to good researchers. No thought is devoted to the possibility of making a Type 1 error, the error that is of withdrawing funding from researchers who would have made important advances if their research had been supported. Yet the history of science shows that Type 1 errors are much more serious than Type 2 errors. The case of Semmelweis is a very striking example. The fact that his line of research was not recognised and supported by the medical community meant that, for twenty years after his investigation, thousands of patients lost their lives and there was a general crisis in the whole hospital system.

In comparison with Type 1 errors, Type 2 errors are much less serious. The worst that can happen is that some government money is spent with nothing to show for it. Moreover Type 2 errors are inevitable from the very nature of research. We can see this by considering again the example involving competing research programmes which we introduced in **3.2**. Suppose research is required on some problem, and there are four different approaches to its solution which lead to four different research programmes. It may be almost impossible to say at the beginning which of the four programmes is going to lead to success. Suppose it turns out to be research programme number 3. The researchers on programmes 1, 2 & 4 may be just as competent and hard-working as those on programme 3, but, because their efforts are being made in the wrong direction, they will lead nowhere. Suppose programme 3 is cancelled in order to save money (Type 1 error), then all the money spent on research in the problem will lead nowhere. It will be a total loss. On the other hand if another programme (5) is also funded, the costs will be a bit higher but a successful result will be obtained. This shows why Type 1 errors are much more serious than Type 2 errors, and why funding bodies should make sure that some funding at least is given to every research school and approach rather than concentrating on the hopeless task of trying to foresee which approach will in the long run prove successful.

4.2 Pink Diamonds

It is sometimes difficult to keep in mind the exact distinction between a type 1 and a type 2 error. This task will, I think be made easier by introducing an analogy. Suppose we have a system for separating flawed diamonds, which have little value, from clear diamonds which are valuable. This system, let us suppose, works very efficiently in eliminating worthless flawed diamonds, but then it turns out to have a crucial defect. As well as eliminating the flawed diamonds, it eliminates the pink diamonds, and pink diamonds have a value a thousand times greater than that of the ordinary clear diamonds. Once our system had been found to have this defect by diamond producers, they would hastily stop using it. My claim is that systems based on peer review, such as the RAE, have exactly the same defect. They are liable to throw away the pink diamonds. The pink diamonds in this case are characters like Frege, and Semmelweis, or, more generally, researchers working on minority research programmes, which are unpopular for the moment, but destined to yield brilliant results in the future. Such people are at risk, in a system such as the RAE, of having their funding or research time reduced, or cut off completely, thereby holding up the progress of knowledge.

I will therefore refer to a serious type 1 error as 'throwing away a pink diamond'. The argument so far can then be summed up by saying that peer review has the defect that it is liable to throw away pink diamonds, and that the same holds *a fortiori* for systems for organising research which, like the RAE, are based on peer review.

4.3 Further Considerations on Peer Review

So far my criticism of peer review has been based on the analysis of historical examples, but it can be extended to include other issues by looking at the contemporary scene. I have had considerable experience of the peer review system over the last 42 years. I edited a major academic journal (*The British Journal for the Philosophy of Science*) from 1982 to 1985 and so sent out many papers for peer review. I have submitted numerous papers to peer reviewed journals and so received numerous referee's reports, and I regularly write quite a number of referee's reports on other people's papers each year. As a result of all this experience, I have formed an idea of which papers are most likely to be accepted and which are most likely to be rejected. My conclusion has been that the type of paper most likely to be accepted is one which 'adds an epicycle' to an existing discussion. Such a paper begins something like this. 'As regards problem area x, the key approach was introduced by A. This was extended by B to cover a further series of cases. C then showed that the combined theories of A and B could be simplified by eliminating the assumption of y. In this paper I will show that C's version of the theory can be extended by adding a new parameter z.' If a paper starts like that, and is technically competent, it can hardly fail to be accepted. The referees may well include at least one, if not two, of A, B, and C. Now A, B, and C are likely to be very pleased with a paper which takes their work seriously and develops it. Let us contrast this with the type of paper which is very likely to be rejected by peer review. Such a paper would begin something like this. 'As regards problem area x, the situation is far from satisfactory. The approach of A, even when extended by B and simplified by C has produced few results, and has not resolved the most important problems. Clearly a new approach is needed and this will be suggested in the present paper.' If A, B, or C are among the referees, they are not likely to be very pleased with such a paper. If it is correct, they were following the wrong approach and their work is likely to be forgotten. Hence the high probability that this paper is likely to be judged by them as a 'crank' approach which should not be taken seriously. There is, however, one further type of paper which is even more likely to be rejected by peer review. This is one which begins: 'The aim of this paper is to propose a new approach to problem area x' and which doesn't even mention the work of A, B, and C. It is widely, and correctly held, that most researchers do not like criticisms of their views. However, what they like even less is for their views to be ignored altogether. This is why the most common comment in a referee's report runs something like this. 'The author fails to mention the important results in the papers A (2000) and A (2005).' A is of course the referee. So common are such comments that it is often easy to guess who the anonymous referee in fact is. A good example of the type of paper which is most likely to be rejected by peer review is Einstein's 1905 paper in which he introduced the special theory of relativity. That paper not only introduces a radically new approach, but does not cite any other paper or book on the subject. One may well wonder how such a paper got accepted for publication at all. I will return to this little historical mystery later on in the book (**9.3**) and give the solution.

There are in fact many other defects in the peer review system. The reviewers tend to be overworked academics who would much rather be getting on with some other work than refereeing a paper which may be on a subject of only marginal interest to them. They are in a hurry to get the job done, and this makes it all the more likely that they will read a difficult paper quickly, and fail to understand it properly. Contemporary journals try to raise standards by increasing the number of referees to whom a submitted paper is sent. However, increasing the number of referees makes it all the more likely that a pink diamond will be thrown away. If there is just one referee, he or she might just possibly be someone of insight who recognises good work in what seems a strange new approach. With 3 referees, at least one is bound to be a conventional thinker who rejects as absurd a new approach.

It is time now to mention a respect in which my analogy with sorting diamonds is not entirely accurate. Diamonds are not changed by the sorting process, but the kind of research produced is changed by the evaluation process. The analysis of the refereeing system which I have just given is well known in the academic world, and the conclusions to be drawn are obvious enough. If you want a paper published in a leading academic journal, you have to choose a well-established discussion, make flattering comments about all the participants so far, and then add an epicycle to their work. Now in order to get a job, and then promotion, researchers need to publish in leading academic journals. Thus most young researchers will follow the strategy just indicated. It was very different with Einstein. He was an ambitious young researcher in 1905, and he tried to develop a new approach to theoretical physics. Unfortunately a young researcher today would almost certainly not succeed with such a strategy, and so most young researchers will not even try such a strategy, even if they would really prefer to do so. In other words, the system is not only likely to reject pink diamonds, but is also very likely to discourage researchers from even trying to become pink diamonds. Isn't this completely wrong? Shouldn't the system encourage young researchers to try to be like Einstein and do something really important? Admittedly many might try to do so, and get nowhere, but a few might really succeed. If all the young researchers are adding epicycles to established research programmes just in order to survive and get jobs, then we are most unlikely to produce new Einsteins.

This conclusion is argued for persuasively by Frey in his 2003. Frey has even more experience of the refereeing system than I can claim. He writes (2003, p. 219):

'I have published more than 350 papers in over 140 refereed journals during the period 1965-2002. Among them are leading economics journals such as *AER*, *JPE*, *RES*, *REcsStats*, *EJ*, *JEcLit* and *JECPersp.*, but also in political science (e.g., *APSR*), psychology, law and sociology journals. ... I have served as one of the two (and later three) managing editors of *Kyklos* since 1970, am a member of the board of editors of 23 journals and over the years have served as a referee for numerous journals.'

This experience has not enamoured him with the refereeing system. He points out another defect of this system. Very often referees demand that the author makes changes to his or her paper. In order to get the paper published, the author has to make these changes even if he or she regards them as completely wrong. Frey regards this as a form of academic prostitution. The title of his paper is: 'Publishing as prostitution? – Choosing between one's ideas and academic success', and he sums up his idea in the paper's abstract as follows (2003, p. 205):

'Survival in academia depends on publications in refereed journals. Authors only get their papers accepted if they intellectually prostitute themselves by slavishly following the demands made by anonymous referees ... . Intellectual prostitution is neither beneficial to suppliers nor consumers.'

The word 'prostitution' is perhaps a bit strong here, but it would be difficult to deny that Frey has exposed a defect in the current refereeing system.

So we can sum up as follows. The main defect of the peer review system is that it is likely to throw away pink diamonds. Moreover, if its use is very widespread, it may create a situation in which researchers, who might otherwise have tried to become pink diamonds, abandon such a strategy just in order to survive in the system. Conversely anyone trying to design a system for organising research should ensure that the probability of throwing away pink diamonds is made as low as possible, and that researchers, particularly young researchers, are encouraged as much as possible to try to become pink diamonds. Surely it is better that at least some young researchers should try to become the next Copernicus than that all young researchers should be forced to resign themselves to a life of adding epicycles to an Aristotelian-Ptolemaic system.

40

Chapter 5. Overall Judgement on the RAE

5.1 Analysis of the Likely Effects of the RAE

Let us begin by considering the effects of the RAE on normal science. In a period of normal science, most of those working in a branch of the subject will accept the dominant paradigm, and no revolutionary alternative will have been suggested. It will then be an easier matter for the experts in the field to judge who is best according to the criteria of the dominant paradigm. Allocating research funding to these most successful 'puzzle solvers', as Kuhn calls them, will usually enable the normal science activity of puzzle solving to continue successfully. One qualification to this must, however, be introduced on the basis of our discussion of research programmes in **3.2**. Suppose there are a number of different research programmes all of which accept the dominant paradigm and so are within normal science. Any system like the RAE which relies heavily on peer reviewing is very likely to concentrate all the resources in those research programmes which are initially accepted by the majority of researchers, while failing to support, or even closing down altogether, minority research programmes. The reason for this is easily seen. The majority of researchers tend to favour the research programme they themselves have adopted, and to regard other approaches as misguided. Thus a set of peer reviewers chosen at random will always tend to favour majority research programmes, while being very critical of minority research programmes.   However, this bias against minority research programmes is very harmful to the progress of research since it has often been the case in the past that minority research programmes have achieved the major advances, whereas majority research programmes have failed to produce any significant results. Obviously this is likely to continue to be the case because research is, by its very nature, so unpredictable.

With this important qualification about minority research programmes, however, we can say that the RAE is not likely to have too damaging an effect on normal science. The only problem is that normal science tends to be routine in character and to produce small advances rather slowly. Surely, however, we want a research regime to encourage big advances in the subject, exciting innovations, breakthroughs, etc. It is precisely here that the RAE is likely to fail. Any major advance is likely to have something revolutionary about it, something which challenges accepted ideas and paradigms. However it is precisely in these cases, as we have shown above, that the RAE with its excessive reliance on peer review is likely to have a very negative effect. Our conclusion then is the RAE is likely to shift the UK research community in the direction of producing the routine research of normal science resulting in slow progress and small advances. At the same time it will have the effect of tending to stifle the really good research – the major advances, the exciting innovations, the big breakthroughs. Clearly then the overall effect of the RAE is likely to be very negative as regards research output in the UK.

The RAE is also likely to impact very negatively on the production of wealth-generating science-based technologies in the UK. The reason for this is that the most striking technologies from the point of view of wealth-generation are often based on revolutionary scientific advances. This is well-illustrated by the three examples considered in chapter 2. Copernicus' new astronomy led, as we have seen, to a much improved navigation, and this was essential to the profitable development of European sea-borne trade in the 17th and 18th centuries. The new mathematical logic introduced by Frege was essential for the development of the computer. It is significant here that Bertrand Russell was one of the first to recognise and develop Frege's work. Russell established an interest in mathematical logic in the UK, which passed on to two later researchers at Cambridge: Max Newman and his student Alan Turing. After the Second World War, Newman and Turing were part of the team at Manchester which produced the Manchester Automatic Digital Machine (MADM). This started running in 1948, and can be considered as the first computer in the modern sense.[6] Thus Russell's early recognition of Frege's revolutionary innovations led indirectly to the UK taking an early lead in the computer field. This early lead was later lost, as we know, but this was owing to lack of sufficient investment by either the public or private sectors. There was no problem with the UK's research community in those pre-RAE days. Our third case concerned the revolutionary introduction of antisepsis in conjunction with revolutionary new theories about the causes of disease. We focussed on Semmelweis whose research work was rejected by the medical community of his time. As we remarked, however, Lister was more successful, and was able to persuade the medical community in the UK to accept antisepsis. This was obviously of great benefit to patients, but I would now like to add that it led to very successful business developments. For his new form of surgery Lister needed antiseptic dressings, and he devoted a lot of time and thought to working out the best design and composition of such dressings. As his ideas came to be accepted, the demand for these dressings increased and companies were formed to produce them. One of these was founded by a pharmacist Thomas James Smith. In 1896, he went into partnership with his nephew Horatio Nelson Smith to produce and sell antiseptic dressings. They called the firm Smith and Nephew. Today Smith and Nephew is a transnational company operating in 33 countries and generating sales of £1.25 billion. The company is still involved in wound care as one of its three main specialities, but it has expanded into orthopaedics and endoscopy. One of its well-known products is elastoplast which was introduced in 1928. The general design of elastoplast is based on some of the antiseptic dressings developed by Lister. The commercial success of Smith and Nephew is a good illustration of the importance of having a satisfactory research regime in the UK. If Lister's research on antisepsis had met the same fate as that of Semmelweis only 17 years earlier, then the firm of Smith and Nephew would not be with us today.

5.2 General Conclusions about the RAE

The RAE is very expensive both in money and in the time which academics in the UK have to devote to it. I have argued in this part of the book that its likely effect is to shift the UK research community in the direction of producing the routine research of normal science resulting in slow progress and small advances, while tending to stifle the really good research – the major advances, the exciting innovations, the big breakthroughs. Thus a great deal of tax payers' money is being spent on an exercise whose likely effect is to make the research output of the UK worse rather than better.

My general argument has brought to light three major faults in the RAE. (1) The RAE rules out the strategy of working for many years on a piece of research before publication. Yet this strategy has proved very successful in the past. We gave Copernicus and Wittgenstein as examples of the success of this strategy, but many other examples could of course be given. (2) The RAE relies too strongly on peer review, which may work not too badly for normal science, but which can give very erroneous results when it comes to the most important revolutionary advances in science. Frege, Semmelweis and Copernicus were all examples of this. (3) The RAE concentrates too much on trying to eliminate Type 2 error, that is the error of funding bad research, but devotes no consideration to eliminating Type 1 error, that is the error of failing to fund good research. Yet Type 1 errors have much more damaging effects on the progress of research than Type 2 errors. This was illustrated above all by the case of Semmelweis where a Type 1 error of failing to recognise and support important research led to thousands of patients dying and a general crisis in the hospitals.

What our critique of the RAE has shown is that research is rather a subtle and complicated activity and that producing a regime in which it flourishes is not an easy matter. Perhaps the biggest difficulty lies in the fact that we cannot tell immediately whether a piece of research is good, and sometimes it is only after a period of as long as thirty years that a fairly definite judgement can be reached. In this respect research differs very strikingly from competitive sports such as tennis or football. We can grade tennis players at a particular moment simply by getting them to play each other in tournaments and seeing who beats who. However, we cannot be sure that a researcher whose work is now judged to be of poor quality may not turn out after all to be a Copernicus, a Semmelweis, or a Frege. Even in cases where it is recognised that a scientific discovery has been made, the importance of that discovery may not become apparent for many years. A good example of this is Alexander Fleming's discovery of penicillin which was made in 1928, and published by Fleming in 1929. Fleming was not harshly treated like Semmelweis or Frege, but the significance of his discovery was certainly not recognised immediately. The head of the laboratory where Fleming worked (Sir Almroth Wright) was a Fellow of the Royal Society and a great admirer of Fleming. In 1930 Wright proposed Fleming for the Royal Society citing his discovery of penicillin and some other research achievements. Fleming, however, was not elected in 1930 or in the four following years. In fact Fleming only became a Fellow of the Royal Society in 1943 when he was 62 years old.[7]

On a more positive note, however, the discussion so far has thrown up some ideas which might be useful to those trying to devise a new system for organising research by showing a way in which their ideas can be tested. Any suggested system for organising research should in my view be subjected to **historical tests**. These tests should consist in taking some leading research achievements from the past, and seeing whether those who carried them out would have fared well under the proposed system. If they would have fared well, the system passes the test. If they would have fared badly, it fails the test and should be altered. In the light of the detailed case histories given in Chapter 2, I will consider the achievements of Wittgenstein (W), Frege (F), and Semmelweis (S), when applying this kind of test, and so speak of the WFS test.

In Part 2 of the book, I will apply the WFS test to the new system with which the government proposes to replace the RAE. This is a system based on metrics. It will be easy to establish that this new system, like the RAE before it, fails the WFS test. In Part 3 of the book, I will show that the alternative system which I propose does pass the WFS test.

Before we come on to this, however, I will give in the next three sections a brief review of some of the other discussions of the research assessment exercise which have appeared so far. This is not intended to be comprehensive, since I may well have missed some interesting material and apologise to any authors who may have made important contributions in this area, but who have escaped my attention. I have already mentioned the work of Bruno Frey in **4.3**, and will mention some further ideas of his later on. I will now consider in turn four other authors: Braben, Charlton and Andras, and Maxwell. All these authors are also critics of the RAE, and their criticisms are quite similar to mine. However, they all use different examples and evidence and so tend to strengthen the case I am presenting. In some cases, however, there may be a difference of emphasis and approach, and I will comment on these differences as I go along.

5.3 Supportive Authors: (i) Braben

Donald Braben's 2004 book: *Pioneering Research. A Risk Worth Taking* does contain criticisms of the RAE, but is more general in scope. It criticises many aspects of research today, and suggests alternative approaches. Braben emphasises the limitations of peer reviewing, writing (2004, p. 70):

' ... *consensual* peer review is inimical to new science. Few major discoveries or inventions are greeted with acclaim. In science, the best of each generation have rarely been quick to recognize what turned out to be the best in the next. That has always been true. Today, however, the all-pervasive peer review bureaucracy is the determinant of excellence, and consequently the natural inclination to oppose major challenges to the status quo has become institutionalized.'

Braben gives a number of examples of cases in which peer review is inimical to new science. As these are different from the examples given above, they add strength to the general criticism of peer review.

One of Braben's examples is perhaps more hypothetical than real. He writes (2004, p. 90):

'John Maddox, *Nature's* very long-serving editor, in his valedictory editorial of December 7, 1995 (p. 521), said:

> It is good joke (which I have often used) that Watson and Crick's paper on the structure of DNA could not be published now. It is only necessary to imagine what people would say if it reached them in the mail: "It's all model-building, just speculation, and such data as they have are not theirs but Rosalind Franklin's!"'

A point which could be added here is that peer reviewing has generally become more rigorous in the last few decades. Whereas formerly one referee working with the editor was often considered sufficient, nowadays two, three or even four referees are used. The use of more referees is designed to make the standard of the papers accepted higher, but, as was pointed out in **4.3** it makes the rejection of pink diamonds more likely.

Braben also mentions the interesting case of Harry Kroto (2004, p. 112):

'The British Member of the trio to discover $60C$ – Harry Kroto of the

University of Sussex – personally had to support some of the crucial early stages of the work. He shared the Nobel Prize for Chemistry in 1996 with Robert Curl and Richard Smalley of Rice University in Houston. In the six years before the prize was awarded, Kroto had a string of applications to EPSRC for substantial funds turned down – one on the grounds that the research was too open ended!'

Braben sums up his general view by saying (2004, p. 166): ' ... virtually every selection protocol used nowadays inhibits adventurous research involving major departures from the beaten tracks.' As a result of this outlook on contemporary research, Braben was anxious to encourage more adventurous research, and actually got a chance to do so. BP decided in 1980 to give his ideas a go, and appointed him as head of a new *Venture Research Unit*. This continued to be funded by BP with Braben as its head until 31 July 1990 when the unit was closed and Braben left BP.

Braben's account of the activities of the Venture Research Unit make fascinating reading, and contains many useful suggestions regarding issues such as the selection of research proposals for funding. However, a word of caution is perhaps needed here. It doesn't seem to me possible to make up for the shortfall in ground-breaking scientific research by setting up special units which specialise in such research. This is for two reasons. First of all it would be very difficult to find funding for such units. Braben remarks that (2004, p. 150):

'The company was "cash rich," as were almost all the oil majors at that time (1979), and BP wanted to invest in the research that might lead to new interests outside its current businesses.'

Moreover he goes on to point out that the Venture Research Unit's budget of £3 million pa, though it may sound large, was very small in relation to BP's annual revenues of about £26 billion. He calculates that the budget was (2004, p.153): 'the equivalent of about an hour of BP's turnover'. All the same, the Venture Research Unit was closed as soon as somewhat more austere times returned for BP. In general, venture research units are only likely to be financed in boom times, and then only to a small extent if at all.

However, there is also a more theoretical argument against the venture research unit approach. It has to be remembered that many important breakthroughs come about because a piece of quite routine normal science has taken an unexpected turn. I will give a very striking example of this in **10.3**, namely Fleming's discovery of penicillin. As we shall see, Fleming was engaged in a standard piece of normal science which went wrong because one of his culture plates became contaminated by a mould. Fleming's brilliance consisted in realising that this accidental occurrence suggested a new line of research which was potentially much more interesting than the one he was carrying out at the time. However, Fleming could never have made an advance application to a venture research unit to enable him to do something unusual.

The approach which I will adopt in what follows is not that of trying to supplement the existing system with some special venture research units, but rather that of altering the existing system so that new research programmes leading to major advances can naturally develop within it without being stifled.

5.4 Supportive Authors: (ii) Charlton and Andras

Charlton and Andras in their 2008 adopt an approach very similar to the one developed here. They argue that the effect of the RAE is to bring about the decline of 'revolutionary science' and the rise of 'normal science' in the UK. Whereas I have argued for this conclusion using historical examples, they do so using scientometric statistics. Thus two separate kinds of evidence support the same conclusion.

Charlton and Andras also introduce the very interesting hypothesis that contemporary UK scientists are 'down-shifting'. They explain this concept as follows (2008, p. 470):

'One hypothesis is that there may have been a "down-shift" strategy of the most able UK scientists to direct their efforts into solving easier and less important scientific problems than they are capable of tackling. ... we suggest that potential UK Nobel prize-winners may, over recent decades, have re-orientated their research away from the riskier strategy of pursuing revolutionary science and towards less ambitious projects that are more immediately productive. In other words we propose that these top UK scientists may – on average – have shifted down a gear, to accelerate their careers by solving more, smaller or easier problems over the short term.'

In an article for *The Oxford Magazine* published in 2008, Charlton elaborates this idea in the context of Oxford scientists. Applying scientometric data, Charlton concludes that Oxford in terms of scientific research is at about the same level as the University of Minnesota. Charlton hastens to emphasize that the University of Minnesota is a very good university by international standards. However, he concludes that Oxford nowadays is not one of the elite universities of the world in terms of scientific research. He attributes this situation to down-shifting brought about by the RAE, writing (2008, p. 4):

'Instead of being urged to take on tough problems where there is a significant chance of failure, the best young Oxford scientists are being pressurized (implicitly for sure, but probably sometimes explicitly) to do easier, more predictable, and more short-term research. Why? Because this is the kind of research which has a higher probability of getting funding, and leading to large numbers of well-cited papers; and all in a timeframe so as to be ready for the next up-coming RAE – with the extra money this brings in.'

There is a certain irony here because Thatcher who introduced the RAE and Blair who continued it were both Oxford graduates. If Charlton and Andras are correct, then Thatcher and Blair did an ill turn to the University where they were educated. In fact, the down-shifting hypothesis of Charlton and Andras does seem to me almost certainly correct, and I will present more evidence for it later on in the book (**10.3** and **11.7**).

5.5 Supportive Authors: (iii) Maxwell

Nicholas Maxwell has made a far-reaching criticism of the research carried out in contemporary universities on the grounds that it is informed by a philosophy of knowledge and that this should be replaced by a philosophy of wisdom. Maxwell discusses the RAE in the second edition (2007) of his book *From Knowledge to Wisdom. A Revolution for Science and the Humanities.* He makes encouraging remarks about my own (2007) paper on the subject, and goes on to reinforce my argument by giving a further series of examples of scientists and mathematicians whose work was not recognised for many years (Maxwell, 2007, p. 317):

'There are many other cases of people making important scientific or intellectual contributions and receiving no recognition for their work for twenty years or more. Thomas Young's discovery of the wave character of light via his interference experiment was initially dismissed by his peers. Gregor Mendel's discovery of some basic laws of genetics famously had to wait several decades before it received recognition. This was true, too, of Alfred Wegener's theory of continental drift, and John Waterston's contribution to statistical mechanics. Georg Cantor met with opposition when he developed set theory – of profound importance to the whole of mathematics. E. Stückelberg failed to receive recognition for his important contributions to quantum field theory. And Guy Callendar failed to convince when he announced in 1938 that increased emissions of carbon dioxide as a result of human activity was leading to global warming. These cases, I am sure, merely scratch the surface.'

Maxwell then goes on to relate the RAE to the question of wisdom-inquiry. Maxwell's general position is that current academic life is dominated by a philosophy of knowledge and that there should be a shift towards a philosophy of wisdom. However, he thinks that the RAE will impede this desirable development, saying (Maxwell, 2007, p. 318): 'It may well be especially difficult for a revolutionary ideas like that of wisdom-inquiry to get a fair hearing in an academic world constrained by the RAE.' Maxwell also gives a striking specific example of a case where the RAE is inhibiting wisdom-inquiry. He writes (2007, p. 317-18):

'But how, it may be asked, may the RAE impede acceptance and implementation of wisdom-inquiry? To begin with, as long as knowledge-inquiry intellectual standards are in place, the RAE will make it even more difficult to do wisdom-inquiry research. The point was made to me in a striking way by Dr. Caren Levy, director of the Development Planning Unit at University College London. Her work and research, like those of others in her Unit, is concerned to help the poor tackle their problems of living in Africa and Asia. Here, if anywhere in academe, wisdom-inquiry is being put into practice. But this creates a dilemma. On the one hand, Dr. Levy can publish papers in relevant academic journals, which gain recognition by the RAE but may not lead to anything of value in the real world. On the other hand, reports produced by Levy, dealing with developmental problems in Africa and Asia, widely read by many grappling with these problems, taken up and implemented by the UN and other organizations, and having practical consequences of value in the real world, receive no recognition from the RAE at all, because the relevant reports are not published in academic journals acknowledged by the RAE. In this way, the RAE increases the pressure on academics to produce orthodox, and often useless, knowledge-inquiry work, instead of really worthwhile wisdom-inquiry work – pressure, I hasten to add, which Levy resists (even if others in other departments do not).'

This criticism of the RAE seems to me entirely correct. Moreover the system proposed in Part 3 of this book as a replacement of the RAE would, I believe, genuinely help researchers like Dr Caren Levy do their valuable work.

It is clear from this that Maxwell and I are in very broad agreement regarding the RAE, and yet there is still, I think, a difference between our positions – even if this difference is perhaps one of emphasis. The difference is this. My own criticisms of the RAE and suggestions for an alternative are based very strongly on considerations which may not have the same weight for Maxwell. These considerations are a desire for *efficiency* and a wish that research should lead to *wealth-generating* innovations. I will make a few remarks about these concepts in the next section.

5.6 Wealth-Generating Innovations and Efficiency

Talk of 'wealth-generating innovations' and 'efficiency' has tended to acquire a bad name because it is associated with philistine politicians who are notably lacking in any concern for cultural values. I too am opposed to such politicians, but their mistake, in my view, is not so much in their general aims as in the erroneous methods they impose for achieving these ends. Thus philistine politicians are apt to recommend that scientists must contribute to wealth generation, and consequently must work only on projects which have an immediate and foreseeable practical application. Of course such a strategy is not a very good one for producing wealth-generating innovations, and indeed often leads to great deal of waste of money. For example, in the development of electronics, the next big step after valves was brought about by the introduction of transistors. This led to a great deal of narrow practical research focussed on improving transistors. There were many research journals devoted exclusively to transistors. However, none of this contributed to the next big step forward which was of course the invention of the silicon microchip. This invention at once rendered all the narrow practical research on transistors valueless, while generating all the wealth of silicon valley.

As we saw the work of Copernicus, Frege and Semmelweis led to wealth generating innovations, but this work was quite different in character from narrow practically focussed research. All three authors initiated revolutions in their fields, and started the process which brought about profound paradigm changes. In fact it is often research of this kind which is the most fruitful in generating wealth.

This point which is so often missed by philistine politicians was well-understood and clearly expounded by Bacon in his *Novum Organum* of 1620. Bacon says explicitly: 'For though it be true that I am principally in pursuit of works and the active department of the sciences, yet I wait for harvest-time, and do not attempt to mow the moss or to reap the green corn.' (1620, p. 251). He believed that in the long run technology could only be improved by improving our knowledge of the natural world, by carrying out basic research in science, as we would now say. In a famous passage, he puts this idea as follows. 'Human knowledge and human power meet in one; for where the cause is not known the effect cannot be produced. Nature to be commanded must be obeyed; and that which in contemplation is as the cause is in operation as the rule.' (1620, p. 259). Bacon makes the same point in another way by contrasting what he calls *experiments of fruit* with *experiments of light*. As he says (1620, p. 245):

'All industry in experimenting has begun with proposing to itself certain definite works to be accomplished, and has pursued them with premature and unseasonable eagerness; it has sought, I say, experiments of Fruit, not experiments of Light; not imitating the divine procedure, which in its first day's work created light only and assigned to it one entire day; on which day it produced no material work, but proceeded to that on the days following.'

Let me turn now to the question of the **efficiency** of a system for organising research. I define the efficiency of such a system as the amount of good quality research produced per dollar, euro, or pound put into financing the system. Here, however, we must be careful. I do not want to suggest that efficiency in this sense can be measured. The denominator of the fraction, that is the amount of money which goes into the funding, can indeed be measured. However the numerator of the fraction, that is the amount of good quality research produced cannot be measured. As has been stressed earlier, it is often impossible to tell whether a piece of research is really of good quality or not until more than thirty years have elapsed. Moreover, even if we look at historical examples and can judge with confidence which bits of research were valuable, it is still impossible to measure the quantity of such valuable research as a number. Given these difficulties, it could well be asked whether the concept of efficiency as just defined is of any use.

I would argue that the concept of efficiency, though qualitative rather than quantitative, is still very useful, for, it enables us to make comparisons between different systems for organising research. Suppose we are comparing two such systems, S_1 and S_2 say. We can first calculate, often quite precisely, the cost of producing so many hours of research work in the two systems. We can then estimate by various indirect considerations which of the two systems is likely to produce more good quality research per hour of research time. If it turns out that S_1 requires more money than S_2 to produce an hour of research time, and if further, S_1 is likely to produce less good quality research per hour than S_2, then we can certainly judge that S_2 is more efficient than S_1. This method will be used in Parts 2 and 3 of this book first to compare the RAE with the system based on metrics with which the government are planning to replace it, and then with the quite different system of research organisation which will be proposed in Part 3.

So, to sum up, my interest in increasing efficiency and helping to promote wealth-generating innovations puts my thinking more in line with the more standard government approach, since almost all governments profess these goals, even if their policies are sometimes a hindrance rather than a help to achieving them. I believe it is the obvious expense and consequent inefficiency of the RAE which has led the UK government to decide to abolish it. In the next part of the book, I will consider the alternative which they have proposed. It will not be difficult to show that this new system will not overcome any of the defects of the RAE, and is likely to be even worse in some ways.

Part 2.

Critque of the New Metrics-Based System

Chapter 6. Would a System based on Metrics be Better?

6.1 Problems with the RAE in 2008

I will rely for my account of the government's new 'metrics based' system on reports in the leading journal of events in the UK's academe, namely the weekly *Times Higher Education* (or THE). Rather confusingly this journal has recently changed its name, and was previously called the *Times Higher Education Supplement* (or THES). So THE and THES actually refer to the same journal. Before examining what future the UK government is planning for its researchers, let us look at some reports in the THE about problems which arose while the RAE was being conducted in 2008. These problems give an idea of why the government decided that RAE 2008 should be the last RAE. By April 2008, the RAE had reached the stage of evaluation. The research material had been collected from up and down the land, and had been handed to the panels to assess. However, THE, 17 April 2008, p. 4 reported a problem:

'Some panels assessing work under the research assessment exercise could find themselves "drowning" under the weight of their workload, ... The average panel member is likely to have to read more than a hundred books or papers between February and September.'

This is a problem with peer review in general, as we mentioned earlier. Academics who already have very heavy workloads may not have time to read the papers they are asked to peer review very carefully. However, this problem seems to have reached an extreme form in the RAE. If the peer reviewers, however well intentioned, have to read dozens of perhaps very difficult papers and books in a limited time, will they always be able to devote the time and attention to each piece which is necessary to judge it fairly? Moreover, the decisions they make will have very serious consequences for some people. Some departments may, as the result of the RAE, have their research funds cut. The members of these departments may have to cancel their research plans, and perhaps some may find their careers ruined.

Given this situation, it seemed very likely that there would be appeals against some of the RAE decisions. Certainly the government anticipated this eventuality as we learn from another article on the same page of the THE (17 April 2008, p. 4). This article is headed: 'Panels ordered to shred all RAE records'. Here is an extract:

'In a confidential letter sent to panel members last November, Ed Hughes, head of the team managing the RAE on behalf of the UK's four funding bodies ... sets out a timetable for the destruction of records. These include personal notes taken by panel members and the panel secretariat, workbooks recording emerging decisions about each submission and draft minutes of meetings.

The letter, leaked to *Times Higher Education*, warns that if academics on the panels make personal notes and hold them for longer than 20 days they may need to be released to comply with legislation if a "relevant request of information" is received.'

It is difficult to see what confidence can remain in the RAE after such revelations. It seems that decisions have to be made in a rush with not enough time allowed to read the submissions carefully, and then all records must be destroyed to prevent any appeals against these decisions.

This situation may indeed have raised some doubts in the government about the RAE, and yet I believe that the main objection of the government to the RAE is probably on the grounds of its expense. For the RAE is indeed very expensive. Extra administrators have to be hired and paid for to carry out all the bureaucracy involved, and most academics have to spend a lot of their time in preparing for the RAE, while other have to spend even more time carrying out the assessment. All this time is of course deducted from what they can spend on the productive activities of research and teaching, thereby increasing the cost of these activities. The 'metrics' plan is essentially designed to retain the general features of the RAE, while greatly decreasing the costs of assessment. Let me now explain how it works.

6.2 The Metrics Approach

The development of computer technology has created vast data-bases containing information about research being carried out. This suggests that instead of getting a panel of humans to judge the value of the research output of a department, one might be able to do it by extracting information from these data-bases, and introducing various measurement formulas, or metrics. We will now consider three of the suggested metrics. The first two of these metrics are, as we shall show, based indirectly on peer review. The third does not involve peer review in its traditional sense.

Perhaps the simplest metric is the following. First all journals in the field in question are assessed as to their academic worth, and given a weighting, say from 5 for the very top and most prestigious journals to 1 for those whose quality is so low as to be barely acceptable. Then the papers published by a given researcher in the period in question are listed and each is multiplied by the weight of the journal in which it appeared. The resulting sum gives a metric for assessing the researcher in that period. Now I think it is obvious that this metric depends entirely on peer review. The weighting of the journals will be carried out by peer review, and the researcher's ability to publish in any of the journals will depend on peer review. Hence the use of this metric would have exactly the same disadvantages of peer review. It would lead to throwing away the pink diamonds etc.

A second metric which has been suggested is to evaluate a department by the amount of research funding it has been able to obtain in the period in question. However, grants are assigned on the basis of peer review, and so this metric once again will have all the defects already noted in peer review. Moreover it is likely to have a further, less immediately obvious, disadvantage which is pointed out by Frey and Osterloh in their 2008, p. 9, namely that 'The tendency to measure research performance by the size of grants received creates an incentive to undertake more expensive, rather than relevant research'. This is a particularly harmful incentive since it goes against the strategy, recommended earlier in **4.1**, of funding a large number of different research programmes in order to ensure that at least one proves successful in solving the problem under investigation.

The third metric we will consider could be called a citation index. It works like this. The value of a paper is assessed by counting the number of times that paper is referred to by other papers in the field. The more the references or citations, the better the research in the paper in question is judged to be. I can illustrate the idea behind the concept of citation index by describing some bibliometric research which I conducted a few years ago (in 2004). I was interested in ascertaining which philosophers were most admired by those who contributed to the well-known UK philosophy journal *Mind* in the period 1991-5. I therefore counted the number of references to authors in *Mind* during those years. I considered articles and review articles, but not reviews. If an author was cited, I counted as separate references only those from separate works by the author. The top 5 authors by number of citations are given in Table 1.

Table 1

The top 5 authors by number of references in Mind in the period 1991-5

	Author	Number of references
1.	Frege	77
2.	Davidson	68
3.	Lewis	67
4=.	Dummett	36
4=.	Quine	36

The curious thing about this table is the following. Those occupying positions 2 to 4= in the table were all then living philosophers occupying eminent positions in the English speaking academic world (Berkeley, Princeton, Oxford, and Harvard). However, the top philosopher by this criterion was none other that Frege who had died in 1925 over 65 years before. I will comment on this result in a moment, but let us now give an analysis of the likely effects of using citation indices as criteria for research excellence.

It is obvious that to receive a lot of citations, a paper must contribute to a research programme on which a lot of other researchers are working. Of course not all papers contributing to such a research programme will get many citations. However, a paper contributing to a research programme on which very few researchers are working is condemned from the start to receive a low rating on a citation index, even if the one or two other researchers on the programme actually give the paper a favourable reception. Hence the use of citation indices to evaluate the quality of research will have exactly the same effect as using peer review. It will encourage researchers to work on the standard paradigms and mainstream research programmes while strongly discouraging them from trying out new approaches and minority research programmes, thus stifling innovations and throwing away the pink diamonds. We can see this easily by applying what I earlier in **5.2** called the WFS test using the example of Frege. How well would Frege have done if a research assessment system based on citation indices been in force in his day? The answer is clearly very badly. In **2.2**, I gave some details of the reception of Frege's works. His 1879 *Begriffschrift* received appalling reviews, his subsequent works of 1884 and 1893 received fewer but equally unfavourable reviews (3 for his book of 1884 and 2 for his book of 1893). Frege's work was completely unrecognised during most of his academic life. Only in the late 1890s and early 1900s did a few avant-garde researchers – notably Peano and Russell – begin to study Frege at all. However, even then, the numbers of those researchers who studied Frege would not have been sufficiently high to give him a good rating on any citation index. So we can conclude that, if a research assessment system based on citation indices had been in force in Frege's life-time, he would have obtained a very low rating, and no doubt have had his research time cut back, thus preventing him from writing those works which led to the Table 1 stellar citation index performance 65 years after his death.

Use of citation indices has another problem which is pointed out in the THES, 23 November, 2007, p.8. A system of research assessment based on citation indices could lead to 'the formation of "citation clubs" in which researchers do deals to cite each others' papers.' Such a development is indeed inevitable in my opinion, and is another example of how introducing criteria of evaluation can change what is evaluated for the worse. A paper whose author honestly cites those other papers which influenced him or her and which he or she thinks to be important can be immensely valuable for other researchers. It gives them an insight into how that author developed his or her ideas and how he or she sees the field. Deviations from this honesty are harmful to the research enterprise. If an author fails to mention, or discusses adequately, a work from which he or she really took some significant ideas, that is obviously plagiarism and is generally condemned. However, it is just as dishonest and harmful for an author to cite works which he or she did not in fact use, and which perhaps he or she actually thinks are really quite bad. Such citations give a distorted and misleading impression of the author's true position. However, as we saw earlier (**4.3**), the peer review system encourages authors to give over-flattering references to those they think might be referees. If citation indices are introduced as criteria for evaluation, then citation clubs will undoubtedly be formed, and the situation will get far worse. Research papers will be loaded with dozens of irrelevant references reducing the quality and usefulness of the papers.

The three metrics which I have discussed so far are the only ones which I have seen suggested for use in the new government system. Moreover, it is difficult to see how there could be others which are not close variants of the ones already considered. Hence we can confidently draw the conclusion that a system based on metrics would have all the defects of the present one based on peer review, and more besides. The additional defects so far discussed are the tendency of researchers to go for unnecessarily large research grants, and the mushrooming of irrelevant and misleading references in papers.

Despite all this, a defender of the new government plan might still maintain that a system based on metrics would at least be cheaper than the existing RAE. Certainly if we are forced to choose between two systems which damage UK research output to about the same extent, then the cheaper one would be preferable! However, the discussions in the THE/THES of how the new metrics system could be implemented strongly suggest that it might not after all be very much cheaper than the RAE.

6.3 Would a Metrics Approach be Cheaper?

At first sight the metrics system appears to be simplicity itself. One need only calculate the value of a few metrics from data-bases and the job is done. In practice, however, things are not so simple as is revealed by Zoë Corbyn's article in the THES on 23 November 2007, pp. 1 & 8. To begin with, it seems that 'Arts and humanities subjects will continue to be judged on the basis of peer review'. For some reason, the citation index is not deemed to be satisfactory for these areas, and will be applied only to the sciences. But how then is comparability between different disciplines going to be achieved? One can foresee many hours of committee time spent on this problem. The same problem also arises within the sciences since different fields have different citation levels. Moreover (p. 1): ' "Suspicious" citation behaviour, designed to manipulate results, will be monitored.' This refers to the "citation clubs" already mentioned. But how is this monitoring to be done? One can imagine many hours of administrative time spent on this problem, and the chances of success appear low.

This was the situation as reported on 23 November 2007, but another article by Zoë Corbyn in the THE on 24 April 2008 shows that things altered over a period of 5 months. Corbyn writes (p. 4):

'In a U-turn announced this week, ministers have abandoned plans to use one system to judge research in the sciences and another in the arts, humanities and social sciences in the forthcoming research excellence framework.'

Corbyn also quotes the following governmental statement (p.4):

'So for all subjects, the assessment will include metrics-based indicators, including bibliometric indicators of quality wherever appropriate, as well as input from expert panels. The balance of metrics and expert input will very according to the subject group.'

What we see emerging is a system of Byzantine complexity which is likely to be even more costly than the original RAE while giving results which are worse rather than better. In terms of the concept of efficiency introduced in **5.6**, the new system will not be more efficient than the RAE, and will probably be much less efficient. Its general effect will be exactly the same as that of the RAE, namely to shift the research community in the direction of producing the routine research of normal science resulting in slow progress and small advances, while stifling the really good research – the major advances, the exciting innovations, the big breakthroughs.

It is also a rather sinister sign that the new metrics-based approach has been given a propagandist name – no doubt devised by some spin doctor. The name of the RAE, i.e. The Research Assessment Exercise, gave an accurate description of what it was designed to do. The name which has been chosen for the new metrics-based approach is *The Research Excellence Framework* (REF). This is clearly designed to imply that the framework will produce excellence in research. However, this implication is most misleading. If the analysis just given is correct, the framework will encourage the production of mediocre rather than excellent research, and it could more accurately be described as *The Research Mediocrity Framework* (RMF).

That concludes my discussion of the new metrics-based approach, and I will now begin considering what alternative way of organising research might be used instead of either the RAE or the RMF. In Part 3 I will make a proposal for such an alternative, and I will compare it in detail to the RAE showing that it would be cheaper and produce better results than the RAE. I will not carry out such a detailed comparison with the RMF because it will be obvious from what has been said in this chapter that the arguments used against the RAE apply just as strongly, if not more strongly, to the RMF. Thus I will, from this point on discuss only the RAE, leaving it to the reader to check that what is said still holds if we substitute the RMF for the RAE.

6.4 Preliminary Sketch of an Alternative Approach

At this point, however, it might begin to seem that there is no way of solving the problem of designing an efficient way of organising research. The key problem is that we cannot properly judge the value of a research contribution until about 30 years after it has been made. Contemporary valuations are shown by history to be very misleading. Contributions which in the perspective of history are seen to be major advances are sometimes judged to be valueless by contemporary researchers. Conversely research which seems brilliant at the time is often seen later to be merely a passing fashion which proved to be of no significance in the long run. If, however, we can only evaluate research properly after 30 years, how can we decide *now* what research to fund. The problem does indeed look insoluble.

But the problem is not really insoluble. All that is needed is a new approach, which I will now explain in outline and then elaborate in Part 3 of the book. What we need to do is to shift our focus away from research to another activity which nearly always accompanies research, namely teaching. So far we have considered the effects of the RAE on the research output of the UK, but what about its effect on teaching in the UK universities? In the next chapter (7), I will argue that the RAE as well as damaging the UK's research output also damages the teaching in UK universities. It is just as bad for teaching as it is for research. However, this result suggests the following idea. The RAE was designed to improve research, but ended up damaging both research and teaching. Suppose now we shift from an attempt to improve research to an attempt to improve teaching. As the results of teaching are more straightforward to assess, this might be an easier problem to deal with. Moreover, if we solve it, it could be that the new system designed to improve teaching might as a spin-off (so to speak) improve research as well. It could be that the connections between teaching and research are such that improving one will result in an improvement in the other, just as damaging one results in damage to the other. I believe that this is really the case, and will show that a system proposed to improve teaching will, as an indirect consequence, improve research as well. This will be done in chapter 8. Then in chapters 10 and 11, I will put forward an exactly parallel claim as regards a third component of the lives of most academics, i.e. administration and management, or admin for short. I will argue that improving admin, which can be done relatively easily, will also have the effect of improving research. So, in a nutshell, the system I propose is designed to improve teaching and admin, and it will be shown that the effect of these improvements will be to improve research as well.

Part 3.

Proposal for a New System of Research Organisation

Chapter 7. Why the RAE makes Teaching Worse

7.1   The RAE gives Monetary Incentives for Research but not for Teaching

There are three separate reasons why the RAE has a bad effect on teaching in the universities, and I will deal with these in turn. The first, and perhaps most obvious reason is concerned with the reward and hence incentive structure introduced by the RAE. Departments get more money if they do well on the RAE, and have their budgets cut if they do badly. However, whether the department's teaching is good or bad has little, if any, effect on its income. In these circumstances, economic rationality dictates that departments should concentrate their efforts on doing well at the RAE, but not bother so much about teaching. Of course humans are not entirely motivated by economic rationality. Many academics feel they have a professional duty to teach the students well, and this sense of duty may counteract the dictates of economic rationality. Still economic rationality is bound to have some effect, and so the incentive structure introduced by the government in the shape of the RAE is bound to have a negative effect on teaching.

Against this argument, it might be pointed out that the government has also introduced an assessment of the quality of teaching in departments. Reviews of departmental teaching are carried out by the QAA or Quality Assurance Agency, and this will ensure, so it could be claimed, that there is no decline in the quality of teaching. The problem here, however, is that there are rewards for doing well on the RAE and penalties for doing badly, but no corresponding rewards and penalties associated with QAA reviews. Hence once again economic rationality dictates not paying much attention to the results of a QAA review.

But why are there are no monetary rewards and penalties for performance on a QAA review corresponding to those for performance on the RAE? Could they not be introduced? A little reflection, however, shows that the two cases are not symmetric. Suppose a department does well on the RAE. It gets a larger budget and this translates into the staff getting more research time and having to do less teaching. Given the present structure of universities, this is interpreted as a reward. Similarly doing badly on the RAE, and hence having less research time, is interpreted as a punishment. But now suppose we wanted to introduce similar rewards and punishments for performance on a QAA review. How could it be done? If a department did well on a QAA review, this should, if the two cases were really parallel, result in the staff having more teaching time. However, unfortunately, this would be interpreted as a punishment, and so departments would endeavour to do badly on QAA reviews in order to escape this punishment. But could we then give more teaching to those departments which did badly on a QAA review, and less teaching to those which did well? This would give the correct incentive for departments to do well on a QAA review, but the net result would be that teaching would be done more and more by those departments which were bad at teaching. This is hardly desirable.

Against this argument it could be objected that there are indirect penalties for doing badly on a QAA review. For example, courses could be withdrawn, the publicity of a bad score on a QAA review might make it difficult for the department to recruit students, and, in extreme cases, the department might be closed down. However, these indirect penalties are hardly as serious a threat for most departments as the withdrawal of funds which results from a worse performance on the RAE. If some courses have to be withdrawn, they can easily be replaced by others. Students in their choice of university are influenced by a host of factors, and the loss of a point or two on a QAA rating might not make much difference to recruiting. As for the risk of the department being closed, this is very remote for a department which is at least reasonably competent. Contrast all this with the situation of a department which had quite a good rating on the last RAE. If this department drops a point or two, it will lose a considerable amount of funding. In these circumstances, it would be quite irrational not to give much more weight to doing well on the RAE than to doing well in a QAA review.

7.2 Departments are Units for Teaching but no longer for Research

Let me now go on to the second reason why the RAE has a negative effect on teaching. This is connected with a curiously out-dated feature of the RAE. The RAE assesses departments, thereby presupposing that departments are the units of research. Now 30 or 40 years ago, that was largely the case. Research schools were indeed principally located in specific departments. However, during the last 20 or so years, this has been completely changed by the development of globalisation. Everyone knows that globalisation has transformed the world economy, and it has similarly transformed research. Typically nowadays research groups, far from being located in single departments, are scattered throughout the world. Their members communicate on a day to day basis by email, and meet regularly at international conferences.

I can illustrate this change by own experiences. When I started research as a graduate student working for a PhD, I joined the Department of Philosophy, Logic and Scientific Method at the London School of Economics in 1966. The head of department was then Professor Sir Karl Popper, and my supervisor was Imre Lakatos. At the time this department was indeed the centre of a very distinctive research school in history and philosophy of science and mathematics. In the last 20 years, I have continued to do research in the history and philosophy of mathematics, but I have never had a colleague in my department who was researching in this particular area. Did this mean I was isolated and had no one with whom to discuss the problems of the field? On the contrary, I have had many more discussion partners in the last 20 years than I did in 1966. The only difference is that, far from being in the same department, they are located all over the world. Of course these days that does not prevent regular discussions by email, and regular meetings in diverse places. This is well-illustrated by listing some of the collections of papers produced by this lively and stimulating group of researchers. I edited one such collection: *Revolutions in Mathematics*, which was published by Oxford University Press in 1992. There were 12 authors – no two of whom were in the same department. By location 1 was from China, 3 from Germany, 1 from Italy, 3 from the UK, and 4 from the USA. However, 1 of those located in Germany was an Italian national, as was one of those located in the USA. As can be seen, we have here a truly multi-national research group. Subsequent collections of papers in this field tell the same story. One published by Kluwer in 2000 was entitled: *The Growth of Mathematical Knowledge*, and was edited jointly by Emily Grosholz of the Pennsylvania State University in the USA, and Herbert Breger of the University of Hannover, Germany. It was the revised proceedings of conferences held in Pennsylvania State University in 1995 & 1996. Next in the series is: *Mathematical Reasoning and Heuristics* published by King's College Publications in 2005. This was edited by Carlo Cellucci of Rome's La Sapienza University and myself. It contains the revised proceedings of a conference held in Rome in 2004. I mention this example from my own experience because I believe that it is typical. The research group based on a single department or university has largely disappeared to be replaced by multi-national research groups. This parallels the increasing transformation of national companies into multi-national companies.

From my own experience I would say that this new form of research organisation is much superior to the old. It allows a much wider range of contacts and discussion partners than did the old system, and this is very important in specialised fields. It also leads to much better human relations within the group, and many less quarrels. If a number of researchers in the same field, but holding different opinions, see each other every day in the same department, the outbreak of quarrels is more or less inevitable. (Such quarrels were a striking feature of the philosophy department at the London School of Economics in the late 1960s.) Moreover the situation is made worse by the fact that members of the same department are often competing against each other for promotion. Discussion by email and occasional meetings cools the situation, and makes such quarrels less likely. Moreover the members of a multi-national research group are not competing against each other for local promotions. Indeed they can help each other to obtain such promotions. If the group as a whole succeeds internationally, its members are more likely to succeed in their own countries. All this leads to a more pleasant and constructive atmosphere within the research group.

Whoever designed the RAE was, however, obviously not aware of these developments, and, as a result, the RAE introduces incentives which have a negative effect. Although university departments are ceasing to be centres for research groups, they remain centres for teaching. Students join a particular department and take most of their courses within that department. If a department is offering degrees in a particular subject, then it is in the students' best interest for it to make appointments in every branch of the subject. Each branch will then be taught by a specialist in that particular field, who will know more about it, and be able to present the results better. This appointments strategy which is best for teaching is, however, undermined by the RAE. If a department wants to do well in the RAE, it has to present itself as being an international leader in some particular branch of research, and this can be achieved by appointing a large number of staff in that branch. So, for example, a mathematics department might appoint researchers in, say, category theory, as half its staff. It can then claim to be a world leader in research in category theory. The problem here is that students taking a mathematics degree in that department do not want half their courses to be in category theory. They want a broad coverage of the subject. This means that the syllabus of the degree offered will be highly distorted, or that half the courses will be taught by people who are not specialists in that field. Either way, teaching is bound to suffer. Many departments in the UK have followed just such an appointments policy in order to shine in the RAE, and this must have had a negative effect on teaching. The irony of the situation is that researchers in a particular speciality are being collected into a single department just at the time when the emergence of globalisation and multi-national research groups makes this quite unnecessary and indeed undesirable. It is interesting to note here how damage to research is going hand in hand with damage to teaching. The RAE is inhibiting the development of the superior multi-national research group, while, at the same time, encouraging an appointments policy which is worse for teaching students.

7.3 The Tale of Ms A and Mr B

I now pass to the third reason why the RAE is damaging teaching in UK universities. I will explain this by a fictional example which is in fact based on a real life case. It will be clear to the reader why I do not want to give the details of the actual characters involved. My fictional characters are a Ms A and a Mr B. Ms A is a good researcher but a bad teacher. She has a brilliant facility for generating new ideas and lines of research. She can quickly turn out papers which are admired by her peers and published in the top journals. Unfortunately, however, Ms A cannot get her ideas across very well to a student audience. She is rather shy and tongue-tied, and cannot understand the difficulty which some students have in grasping points which to her are obvious. Mr B is exactly the opposite. He is highly studious, and knows his subject well. Unfortunately though, he just doesn't seem to get many new ideas when it comes to research. Moreover while Ms A can dash off a research paper in a couple of days, for Mr B writing is a slow and painful process and he may take months to complete a short article. On the other hand, once in front of a class of students, Mr B is in his element. He speaks well with a great command of rhetoric. He is a charismatic figure loved by the students, and expounds even the hardest points so clearly that every one can understand them. In this fictional example, based on reality, common sense obviously dictates that Ms A should do more research and less teaching, while Mr B should do less research and more teaching. Before the RAE, such an arrangement would without doubt have been made informally. I will now show, however, that a desire to perform well on the RAE could lead to exactly the opposite allocation of research time.

The rules of the RAE have varied over time, but in most RAEs, including the 2008 one, there has been an upper limit to the number of publications (papers or books) which an individual member of staff can submit. In the 2008 RAE the limit was 4. Moreover the more members of staff of a department who can submit to the RAE, the better the rating of the department is likely to be. Now suppose, to continue our fictional narrative, that there is a five year period from the last RAE to the next one, and that a year and a half has elapsed. The prodigious Ms A has already completed 4 brilliant papers, while Mr B the poor researcher and slow worker hasn't even managed to complete one. The head of department now considers what must be done to get the best rating for the department at the next RAE. Ms A has already completed all that needs to be done, and to a very high standard. Thus there is no point in giving her more research time. Mr B is a slow coach, but, if he is given a lot of extra research time, he might just manage to get the necessary 4 papers completed. Thus the rational policy for doing well on the RAE is to cut Ms A's research time and give her more teaching, while allocating more research time and less teaching to Mr B. Thus the requirements of the RAE lead to a strategy which makes the teaching much worse for the students, and, at the same time, reduces the quality of the department's research output.

Having shown that the RAE reduces the quality of teaching, I will argue in the next chapter that measures to improve teaching will have a positive effect on research as well.

Chapter 8.   Why Rewarding Teaching will Improve Research

8.1 Limitation to Non-Laboratory Research

This is the chapter in which I will give an outline of a scheme of research organisation designed to be an alternative to both the RAE and the new approach based on metrics. Naturally I will not try to develop the scheme in enormous detail, but will try to bring to the fore its main features so that they can be contrasted with existing approaches. Nor will I try to present a scheme designed to cover all types of research, but will consider only non-laboratory research. This might seem a rather severe limitation since the popular image of research is of white-coated scientists working in a laboratory. However, non-laboratory research is in fact quite an extensive area. It includes all of the humanities such as history, literary and linguistic studies, philosophy, etc. It also includes a good deal of the social sciences, and in particular most of sociology and economics. Then there are disciplines such as mathematics, theoretical physics and computer science. I have two reasons for limiting myself to non-laboratory research. First of all it is the simpler case to consider, and thus is the more natural starting point for trying to devise a system for organising research effectively.   It is simpler because the equipment needed, such as libraries, computers, etc., is automatically provided in any university. Thus the problem is only that of allocating research time to members of staff. Laboratory research involves additional, and often very expensive, equipment.   So there is the further problem of deciding what pieces of such equipment should be purchased. The second reason why I will not consider laboratory research is that I have never taken part in such research either as an individual or as part of a joint project. By contrast I have carried out a great deal of non-laboratory research which has been mainly in my own subject (history and philosophy of science and mathematics), but has also involved working on interdisciplinary research projects with computer scientists, mathematicians, and economists. My long years of carrying out research (so far 42 in number) have taught me that research is a strange activity which often works in quite counter-intuitive ways. Thus it is highly dangerous for anyone without direct experience to suggest rules for how research should be organised. As I lack experience of laboratory research, I prefer not to discuss it. However, I do think that some of the principles developed in this paper for non-laboratory research could be extended to laboratory research, and I hope that someone who is sympathetic to the approach and has experience of laboratory research will carry out this extension.

8.2 The Three Activities of Academics

The vast majority of non-laboratory research is carried out in universities by academics who are not exclusively research workers. In fact these academics generally have 3 rather different activities in their work, namely (1) research, (2) teaching, and (3) administration and management (which I will abbreviate to admin). There are typically 4 grades in the academic hierarchy. Academics start at the lecturer grade, and can then, if they are fortunate, obtain promotions to senior lecturer, reader, and finally professor. Most universities internationally have four grades of this type, though they often have different names. As regards obtaining promotion, however, there is a very striking difference between the 3 academic activities just listed. Promotions can be obtained for either research or admin, but rarely, if ever, for teaching. An academic who concentrates on teaching might, if he or she is lucky, obtain a promotion from lecturer to senior lecturer, but, generally speaking, that is as high as he or she can hope for. To get to a readership or professorship, success in research or admin is what counts. Typically someone might be at the reader grade, and then after taking on an important admin job, such as head of department, would obtain a professorship. Of course professorships are sometimes obtained just by success in research with little admin activity. However, admin is usually a better bet than research for climbing the ladder. The highest grade a research specialist is likely to obtain is professor, while a specialist in admin can go to higher and better paid jobs such as dean, pro-vice-chancellor, or even head of the whole university.

I remarked earlier that teaching is at present of low status in UK universities, and having to do more teaching is usually regarded as a punishment. This is not, I claim, because teaching at university level is an intrinsically unpleasant or unrewarding activity. Quite the contrary is the case. Teaching bright students who give a stimulating feedback, preparing new courses covering the latest discoveries in the field, etc., all these can be very enjoyable and intellectually demanding. Indeed, generally speaking, teaching is a much more interesting activity than admin. Still ambitious and talented academics prefer to do research or admin, and this is for the obvious reason that work in research or admin can enable a person to climb the status hierarchy, while work in teaching cannot.

How can this situation be put right? There is an obvious way. The criteria for promotion must be altered so that it is just as easy, or perhaps even easier, to climb the ladder by working as a teacher as by working at research or admin. Actually it is much easier to assess a person's performance as a teacher than to assess someone's performance as a researcher. The quantity of teaching carried out in terms of number of hours and number of students is immediate. As usual, an assessment of quality is more problematic, but not nearly as problematic as is the case with research. One can use student feedback, and exam results. Then there are more subtle and important criteria, such as those of introducing new teaching methods, up-dating courses to contain the latest results in the field, and so on. However, unlike the case of research where a long period is needed to assess the worth of a piece of work with any confidence, the assessment of teaching can be done contemporaneously.

Note, however, that I am not arguing for teaching-only posts. In fact I will argue against such posts in a moment. My argument is that an academic's teaching activities should count just as much towards promotion as his or her research and admin activities. If this were to happen, the status of teaching would rise, and the quality of teaching would improve. I will next show that this would also improve the quality of research.

8.3 Outline of the Proposed System

I will now give an outline of the system I propose. As we have seen, academics have 3 activities between which they divide their time, namely (1) research, (2) teaching, and (3) admin. The problem is how research time should be allocated. The RAE attempts to solve this problem along the following lines. An assessment is made of how good academics are at research and those who are better are allocated more research time. There are two fundamental difficulties with this approach. First of all carrying out the assessment is very costly, and secondly its results are very dubious. It is perfectly possible that someone who is really a brilliant researcher could get a low rating on the assessment, and hence be prevented from doing research, thereby throwing away a pink diamond. Instead of this approach, I therefore propose that academics themselves should decide whether they want to do more research, more teaching, or more admin. This I call the principle of **self-selection**. It will be seen at once that this principle solves both the main problems besetting the RAE. First of all it becomes unnecessary to carry out a complicated assessment of all researchers, and so there are enormous cost savings. Secondly, the risk of committing a type 1 error (throwing away a pink diamond) is reduced almost to zero. It is not possible to recognise the pink diamonds of research immediately, but they all have one characteristic in common. They love research and are very keen to do it. Thus, given a principle of self-selection, they would all go for the research option.

However, at this point, many readers will perhaps smile and conclude that I am proposing a purely utopian scheme which has an obvious flaw. Surely the objection will be made, if a principle of self-selection is adopted, everyone will opt for research whether they are pink diamonds or plain incompetents, and so it will be impossible to get any teaching or admin done. This objection has an apparent force because there is a certain hypocrisy in academic circles.

I have yet to meet an academic who did not claim that what he or she really loved best was research. However, observing the behaviour of those who make such professions, one has to conclude that they are often false. Academics typically start with great enthusiasm for research, but, after a number of years working at research, they often become rather bored with it. They may have run out of ideas. They may have come to realise that their youthful hopes of becoming the next Einstein were an illusion, while the reality is that there are quite a number of younger researchers doing better than they are. In these circumstances the sensible move is into administration and management where a tempting career ladder stretches before them. Indeed many who do switch from research to admin may have carried out quite a lot of brilliant research, but do not think they are capable of continuing. This is often the case with mathematicians who characteristically make their best contributions when young. Several eminent mathematicians who have proved deep theorems in their youth switch in middle life into administration and management and are often successful at that as well. In so doing they are following in the footsteps of the great Sir Isaac Newton. His masterpiece *Principia Mathematica* was published in July 1687 when its author was 44. However, Newton did not spend the rest of his life carrying our research in mathematics and physics, but rather switched into a new career in administration and management, not in Cambridge University but at the Royal Mint in London. He became Warden of the Royal Mint in 1696, and was promoted to Master in 1699. Apparently he ran the Royal Mint very well.

What I am saying is that many academics would be quite happy to switch their activity away from research provided they do not lose any status thereby and indeed have instead the chance of climbing a career ladder. Given the present set-up, such academics will choose the admin path and shun teaching which gets nowhere. However, if a switch into teaching could lead to a successful career, many academics would be happy to follow that path, and indeed many might much prefer it to the admin path.

These considerations lead to the following outline of my suggested system. A young academic is given a first appointment with a fairly generous allowance of research time. Later on, however, he or she can decide whether to continue with that amount of research time or to switch to doing more teaching or more admin or more of both. The incentive to doing less research and more teaching or admin would be that it would make it easier to obtain promotion and extra money. Obviously the easier it was to gain promotion and extra money by doing say teaching, the more academics would choose the teaching option. Hence the difficulty of getting promotion in the various kinds of academic activity could be adjusted empirically, so that, overall, the required amount of research, teaching and admin was carried out. To put it another way, academics would be tempted into doing more teaching and less research by the possibility of climbing the ladder more easily in this way, rather than, as in the present system, prevented from doing research because their department obtained a low rating on the RAE.

8.4 Arguments against Teaching-Only or Research-Only Posts

However, though some academics would do less teaching and more research and others more teaching and less research, I would argue that all academics should do some of both. I strongly oppose the idea of teaching-only posts for the simple reason that they would result in a decline in the quality of teaching. Suppose someone is appointed to a teaching-only post. In the first few years he or she might be excellent, but, after twenty years, the subject would have moved on. With no research time to study the new developments our 'teacher-only' would inevitably have become out of date, and his or her teaching would suffer. Besides this, teaching in the final year of an undergraduate degree and at master's level involves setting students research projects, and a teacher with no links to research would be unable to do this satisfactorily. The situation would be made even worse by the creation of teaching-only universities.

So, if we want to improve teaching rather than make it worse, it is necessary that every university teacher should have an allocation of research time. This time need not necessarily be used for writing new papers and books (what could be called 'active research'). It could be used for studying the latest developments in the field, attending research seminars etc (what could be called 'study research'). Obviously carrying out active research requires also carrying out study research, but it is possible to do only the latter.

Conversely I believe that all researchers should do some teaching. It is very helpful to any researcher attempting to formulate new ideas to try to expound them to a student audience. Incomprehension by the students can be an incentive to improve the clarity of the formulation, while often students make critical comments and useful suggestions which lead to an improvement of the content of the research.

Thus all academics should do some research and some teaching, but it is perfectly legitimate and indeed desirable that some should do more research and less teaching while other should do more teaching and less research. Remember the story of Ms A and Mr B given in **7.3**.

We have already indicated how promotions could be based on the quantity and quality of teaching. Promotions on the basis of admin could remain as they are now, while promotions for those specialising in research would be based on peer review carried out in a manner to be explained in the next chapter (Chapter 9). It may seem that, after all my criticisms of peer review, it is a bit inconsistent of me to re-introduce it at this point. However, as I will explain in the next chapter, peer reviewing used in this context in the manner to be described will not lead to the problems occasioned by the way it is used at present.

8.5 Application of the WFS Test to the Proposed System

Let us now apply the WFS test to this suggested system. How would Wittgenstein, Frege and Semmelweis have fared in the proposed system? In fact all three would have been allowed to continue their research. Wittgenstein by refusing to publish anything would have failed to obtain promotion and so remained at a low grade. However, this would have suited him very well. Although heir to one of the largest fortunes in Europe, he gave all his money away and liked to live in what can only be described as 'ostentatious poverty'. To have a low-grade and poorly paid academic job would have suited him down to the ground. Frege's fate under the suggested system would be much what it was in real life. He was never recognised by his academic peers during his years at Jena university and in fact was never promoted to the highest grade (Professor Ordinarius). As it took nearly 40 years for his work to become generally recognised, then, in the suggested system, he would have had great difficulties in getting promotion on the basis of peer review, but he would still have been allowed to continue his research. However, Frege is really exceptional from this point of view. While it is not so uncommon for innovators to have to wait some years for their work to be recognised, the number of these years is usually less than twenty or thirty, so that an innovator who, like Frege, produced a great research work at 31 would usually have received enough recognition to climb to the top of the promotion ladder before retiring at 65. Semmelweis died at only 47, but had he lived to be 60, i.e. until 1878, he would have seen his approach become generally accepted by the medical profession, and would, without doubt, have had all the honours, promotions, and acclaim which he failed to obtain because of the shortness of his life. So we can conclude that the suggested system passes the WFS test which is so strikingly failed both by the RAE and the proposed new system based on metrics. As it would also be much cheaper than either of these two systems, it must surely be judged to be superior. Still there are bound to be objections to the system just suggested, and I will now go on to consider some of them.

8.6 Objections to the Proposed System: (i) it might encourage Idleness

The first objection which might be raised concerns the following feature of the system proposed. Academics in this system could opt choose to do more research and less teaching at a young age, and continue in that position for the rest of their working lives despite always receiving bad reports about the quality of their research from their peers. Of course this feature of the system is essential because it is designed to prevent throwing away pink diamonds. However, it could be objected that such a system could well be exploited by academics who, far from being pink diamonds, were idle scoundrels. Such academics might opt for research time with no intention of ever doing any research, and indeed might use their free time on other lucrative activities.

A little reflection, however, shows that no such consequences are really to be feared. First of all there could, and should, be strict rules forbidding academics who have taken a largely research position indulging in any other form of gainful activity, except with special permission from their employer. Those breaking such a rule would lose their academic position. Secondly though it is very difficult to check whether someone is actually producing good research, because of the difficulty of judging what is good research, it is very easy to check whether that person is trying to do research. In **1.3**, I discussed the example of Wittgenstein, who refused to publish anything in his last 17 years of academic life (1930-1947). However I observed that during this period he produced an average of 26 pages of manuscripts or typescripts on philosophy per week. Thus, if Wittgenstein had been asked to produce some of his manuscripts or typescripts for inspection, he could very easily have demonstrated his industriousness. Of course Wittgenstein himself would not doubt have been very offended at such a request, but lesser mortals would probably be only too happy to comply.

Thus there is no real danger of those who hold a largely research position, idling their time away, or holding that position and using the time available to do things other than research.

8.7 Objections to the Proposed System: (ii) it might waste Money on Incompetents

However, a more sophisticated objection could perhaps be raised at this point. There might, so it could be claimed, be academics who believe that they are brilliant researchers, but are really total incompetents. Such academics might indeed work hard for many years, but only produce a lot of rubbish which no one will ever want to look at. It might be claimed that the system I am advocating will produce a lot of rubbish of this sort at tax payers' expense.

Now I certainly do not deny that there are people who believe themselves to be brilliant researchers when they are not so at all. Indeed to reinforce this point, I will give a historical example of such a person. This comes from Bruce Kuklick's admirable 1977 book: *The Rise of American Philosophy.*

Cambridge, Massachusetts, 1860-1930. Kuklick deals at length with the great philosophers of that period such as Charles Sanders Peirce and William James. However, an interesting feature of his book is that he also mentions some figures who were failures rather than successes. One of these was a man called: Frank Abbot.

Frank Abbot was born into an old New England family in 1836, and went to Harvard in 1855. He had some problems relating to his fellow students, and (Kuklick, 1977, p. 92) 'he confessed to them that he had worn a pair of fake glasses to look intellectual'. Abbot tried to start an academic career in philosophy in the mid-1860s, but was rejected by Cornell, Harvard, M.I.T., and John Hopkins (Kuklick, 1977, pp. 92-3). In the 1870s, he proposed to the President of Harvard, Charles Eliot that a research professorship be created for him at Harvard. The details were as follows (Kuklick, 1977, p. 93):

'Abbot would fund the chair for five years and then the university would support him for life if, as he predicted, he came up with a book for the ages that would redound to the glory of Harvard and of the United States. Of course Abbot was unsuccessful – Eliot said he would damage the school's reputation – and ... he was forced in the 1880s to convert his home into a boarding school for boys preparing for Harvard ...'

In order to get students for his school, Abbot obtained a Harvard PhD in 1881, and he claimed (Kuklick, 1977, p. 93) that 'His dissertation ... was "the gist of the greatest philosophical system since the *Critique of Pure Reason* was published in 1781"; men would value it for "hundreds of years to come."' Earning his living from his school, Abbot continued his researches with great vigour, publishing *Scientific Theism* in 1885, and *The Way Out of Agnosticism; or the Philosophy of Free Religion* in 1890. His wife to whom he was much attached died in 1893, and Abbot resolved for her sake to finish a philosophical magnum opus. Kuklick recounts Abbot's tragic and touching final days as follows (1977, pp. 101-2):

'Toward the end of 1903 he had completed a manuscript of over a thousand pages. On September 29 he wrote in his detailed personal diary, "A life-task done ... . At a quarter past twelve, midnight, I finished the last page. ... I shall never reap a harvest from this seed – may it feed a world famine-struck for truth! ... I have fought the good fight. *Nunc Dimittis*." On October 22 he took a bouquet of carnations to his wife's grave and there, sometime in the early morning of October 23, exactly ten years after her death, he poisoned himself.

Three years later in 1906 Abbot's son published the two-volume *Syllogistic Philosophy; or Prolegomena to Science*. He sent the book to every major library in the land. Though it was "the burden of his life," Abbot's work, filled with his own terminology, did not make the slightest impact on philosophical and theological tendencies in the United States.'

It is interesting to note the parallels between Abbot and Frege. Frege published his *Begriffsschrift* in 1879, while Abbot finished his Harvard PhD dissertation in 1881. Both Frege and Abbot aimed to criticize and develop Kant. Both continued working on their philosophy in the 1880s despite a total lack of recognition. Frege finished his magnum opus (*Grundgesetze der Arithmetik*) in 1903, the same year in which Abbot finished his final work. To judge by the title of this work of Abbot's, it must have involved some kind of logical system. All these similarities show how difficult it is to distinguish the genuine pink diamond (Frege) from someone who was not after all a pink diamond, but believed himself to be one (Abbot).

However, to return to our main theme, a critic might object that my proposed system would result in government money being wasted on supporting a large number of Frank Abbots. To this criticism I reply as follows.

First of all Frank Abbots are very rare – much rarer even than pink diamonds such as Frege. Naturally most researchers are disposed to think well of their own research. This is just human nature. However, to sustain the illusion that rather mediocre research is in fact brilliant over a period of twenty or more years goes far beyond this normal human propensity. Such self-deception is very unusual. Most researchers have a rather more realistic assessment of the value of what they are doing. If, after a number of years of research work, they have produced nothing that is admired by their peers, they are likely to draw the probably correct conclusion that what they are doing is not very outstanding. They may indeed have reached the conclusion that others are getting better results. They may have run out of ideas for further research, and indeed be rather bored with research. At this point, it may begin to seem unlikely that they will ever reach the top of the ladder if they stick to a primarily research post, and they may welcome the possibility of other ways of advancing their career. If this were not so, why would so many academics switch from research to admin? If teaching is rewarded in the same way as admin, many will switch to teaching. Thus, the number of Frank Abbots will remain very low. Secondly, even those few Frank Abbots, will, by definition, remain at the lowest point of the scale, for, since their work is not recognised by their peers, they will never gain promotion. Hence the money spent on Frank Abbots will be very low. Finally the error of funding a Frank Abbot is of course a Type 2 error, and no system can avoid Type 2 errors. In fact a Frank Abbot kind of Type 2 error would be a very uncommon one. The usual way in which Type 2 errors arise is, as has already been pointed out (**4.1**), the following. There is a particular research problem to be solved, and four different approaches to this problem. Later it is discovered that only approach number 3 leads to a solution. Initially, however, all four approaches look very promising. Those researchers who choose approaches 1, 2 & 4 may be very talented and hard-working, but all their efforts will lead nowhere. In retrospect we could say that funding approaches 1, 2 & 4 was a Type 2 error. From this it is clear that Type 2 errors cannot be eliminated, any more than it would be possible to ensure, when looking for oil, that every hole drilled produced oil. It is part of the nature of research that Type 2 errors must occur, and there is no reason why the principle of self-selection here proposed should produce any more Type 2 errors than other principles of selection.

8.8   Objections to the Proposed System: (iii) it is Utopian and Unworkable

Let us turn now to another, more general, objection. The system I propose depends on two related principles. Principle 1 is the principle of self-selection, i.e. academics themselves choose if they want more research time. The choice is not imposed on them by allegedly more knowledgeable managers. Principle 2 is that teaching is raised in status through being better rewarded. Obviously the two principles go together, for, if teaching remains an activity of low status which is poorly rewarded then no one is going to choose it in preference to research, even if they do actually prefer teaching to doing research. However, at this point, a critic might object that teaching will never acquire the same status as research, and so the whole scheme proposed is utopian and unworkable. My answer to this objection is to produce a historical example of a system which was very successful at producing high quality research over a long period, and in which the two principles just stated were actually embodied. Since such a system did actually exist, this shows that my proposal is perfectly workable and cannot be dismissed as utopian.

My historical example is Cambridge, UK in the period 1897 to 1953. The starting and ending dates are here somewhat arbitrary. They are chosen because 1897 is the date usually given for J.J.Thomson's discovery of the electron, and 1953 for the elucidation of the structure of DNA by Crick and Watson. For this reason, I will refer to Cambridge in this period as Cambridge (Electron to DNA).

The life of academics in Cambridge (Electron to DNA) is described in an entertaining book by Noel Annan (*The Dons*, 1999). Actually the scope of Annan's book is rather wider. He covers both Oxford and Cambridge, goes back further into the 19th century and takes the story down to Margaret Thatcher whose changes effectively brought an end to the *ancien régime*. Cambridge (Electron to DNA) is certainly within living memory, and yet Annan's account describes a society which seems now as remote as that of the Middle Ages. Annan dwells lovingly on the witty remarks and eccentric behaviour of a class of dons who seem to indulge themselves in a privileged and leisurely existence. One can almost begin to sympathise with the wish of Thatcher and Blair to do away with all these frivolous idlers and modernise an archaic institution. Yet when the research output of Cambridge (Electron to DNA) is examined, it turns out that first impressions are misleading. These seemingly frivolous idlers actually produced a quite stunning quantity of brilliant research over a period of more than 50 years. Moreover this research was not in just one field but in nearly all fields. I will now give a brief survey.

In philosophy, there was Russell's development, with Whitehead, of the logicist view in the philosophy of mathematics. G.E.Moore wrote a masterpiece of ethical theory. Keynes as young man produced his well-known treatise on probability, which was later, in the 1930s, eclipsed by his still more striking contribution to economics in the *General Theory*. Ramsey, the prodigy who died in 1930 at the age of only 26 made major contributions to probability, mathematical logic, philosophy of mathematics and even economics. Wittgenstein started as a pupil of Russell's in his youth, and then, later on produced, an entirely new philosophy in the period 1930-47. In literary criticism, there was the towering figure of Leavis who produced his major books in the period. Leavis published *New Bearings in English Poetry* in 1932, and in the same year founded the periodical *Scrutiny* of which he was the chief editor until 1953. In 1948 he published his views on the novel in English in *The Great Tradition*. In mathematics Turing published in 1936-7 his famous paper entitled: 'On Computable Numbers with an Application to the *Entscheidungsproblem*' which became the theoretical foundation of the modern digital computer.

So far I have discussed non-laboratory research, on which we are focussing. However laboratory research was just as successful in Cambridge (Electron to DNA). The main centre for such research was the Cavendish laboratory which was initially headed by J.J.Thomson who won the Nobel prize for his discovery of the electron. He was succeeded by another Nobel prize winner: Rutherford. Under Rutherford's direction, the year 1932 proved to be an *annus mirabilis* for the Cavendish. Chadwick discovered the neutron, while Cockcroft and Walton split the Lithium nucleus. Chadwick, Cockcroft and Walton were all awarded the Nobel prize, while further Nobel prizes came to Francis Aston, Lawrence Bragg, and Charles Wilson (c.f. Annan, 1999, pp. 122-3). Nor was theoretical science neglected at Cambridge (Electron to DNA). Paul Dirac made remarkable contributions to the development of quantum theory and predicted the positron. He too won the Nobel prize. Moreover the achievement of those further Nobel prize winners Crick and Watson in elucidating the structure of DNA can also be considered as a theoretical achievement, though it was closely connected to experimental work.

More than 50 years have passed since the ending of Cambridge (Electron to DNA) so that we can now judge with confidence that the research produced at Cambridge in that period was not only great in quantity but outstanding in quality and of permanent value. Yet Cambridge in those days was a small university which did not have very large grants. Thus this large amount of high quality research was actually produced for a relatively small amount of money. In effect Cambridge (Electron to DNA) was a very efficient research organisation – perhaps the most efficient which has ever existed. The study of Cambridge (Electron to DNA) should therefore be of interest to anyone who wants to design an efficient system for producing good quality research.

However, here we must sound a note of caution. In the study of any intellectual flowering such as Cambridge (Electron to DNA) it is very difficult to distinguish features of the system which had an important causal role in bringing about the flowering from those which were only incidental. For example, in Cambridge (Electron to DNA), the dons wore gowns and sometimes even mortar boards. In splendid academic attire, they participated in medieval ceremonies which were often conducted in Latin. Now I have no wish to disparage these quaint customs which have an undoubted charm, but it also seems to me clear that they had little effect on the quantity and quality of the research produced. Moreover the causal factors which led to the flowering are unlikely to have been all internal features of Cambridge University itself. Surely features of the wider society must have been very important.

My aim, however, is not to attempt a causal explanation of the success of Cambridge (Electron to DNA), but rather to use this historical example as a means of testing out the principles which underlie proposed systems for the organisation of research. Suppose, for example, some principle is claimed to be necessary for the production of good quality research. If it can be shown that this principle was not applied at all in Cambridge (Electron to DNA), the case for it being necessary is obviously strongly undermined. Conversely if other principles are claimed to utopian and impractical, this claim is undermined if it can be shown that those very principles were indeed adopted in Cambridge (Electron to DNA). The same methodology could be applied using other examples of intellectual flowerings.

One principle clearly underlies both the RAE and the suggested successor systems based on metrics. This is the principle that researchers have to be regularly assessed to make sure they are performing well. This principle has considerable appeal to common sense, because it would seem that if researchers were paid money to carry out research without being assessed, they would just pocket the money without doing anything. It would not be difficult for a media tycoon to convince the general public of the truth of this principle by running a media campaign in its support. Yet the example of Cambridge (Electron to DNA) strongly suggests that the principle is completely false. In Cambridge (Electron to DNA) there was of course no government imposed assessment of researchers such as the RAE, but one can further say that there was no assessment of researchers at all. Yet the researchers of Cambridge (Electron to DNA), instead of lapsing into idleness, produced research which was remarkable both for its quantity and quality.

8.9 The Principles here advocated were embodied in Cambridge (Electron to DNA)

As I have already pointed out, my own proposed system of organising research is based on two principles: the principle of self-selection, and the principle of according high status to teaching. I will now establish that these principles are not utopian and impractical by showing that they were actually embodied in the social practice of Cambridge (Electron to DNA). This can be most easily done by considering a particular case, and I have chosen as my example an English don at King's College Cambridge in this period, namely George Rylands. Details about the life and activities of George Rylands are to be found in Annan, 1999, Ch. IX, pp. 170-192, and in the Memoir edited by Peter Jones which was published in 2000 by Rylands' college after his death.

George Rylands was in fact always known as Dadie Rylands. He was elected to a fellowship at King's College Cambridge with a dissertation on Mallarmé's reply to Degas. This was published as a book entitled: *Words and Poetry* in 1928. Dadie Rylands remained a fellow of King's College Cambridge for the rest of his life, but published no further books and very few papers indeed. This fact alone must fill the contemporary reader with surprise. Nowadays a man with such a publication record would surely be dismissed from his post. Indeed Dadie Rylands' great admirer, Noel Annan, acknowledges this, writing (1999, pp. 187-8):

'When … the government imposed … demands for evidence that dons were "productive", what would the … Committee have made of Rylands' pursuits …? … Would the idea that he had enhanced the culture of the country have crossed their minds?'

Things, however, were different in Cambridge (Electron to DNA). Dons were under no obligation to be research active. They could choose to do research and publish books and papers, but equally they could choose not to do so. This can be clearly seen by comparing Rylands with his contemporary Leavis. Leavis was extremely energetic in writing books, publishing papers, and editing a journal. Rylands did very little of any of these things. This example shows that the principle of self-selection applied in Cambridge (Electron to DNA).

It was not, however, that Rylands was an idler. To begin with, while he did not do much active research in the sense of writing papers and books, he did a great deal of study research. Peter Jones who edited the memoir of Rylands for King's College Cambridge, recalls (2000, p. 3) that 'A particular thrill, happily many times repeated, was to be given a guided tour around his books and collections.' Dadie Rylands' teaching was informed by a thorough knowledge of the contents of his vast library, and this teaching seems to have been very successful, as is shown by the account of Rylands' lectures in 1942 by Anthony Brett-James. I will quote from this at length as it gives a vivid impression of Dadie Rylands in action. (Jones, 2000, pp. 25-26):

'George Rylands of King's was the only don at Cambridge whose lectures I admired. ... Dramatic in every movement, G.R. would arrive late, pushing majestically though the swing doors ... open his notes, and arrange on the desk before him the handful of books that he invariably brought to lectures, marked with slips of paper, and from which passages were read as the hour passed. ... 'The background to the Victorian Novelists' was the subject that he treated in such masterly fashion – a vast picture of the social, political and economic life of the 19th century in Britain, as far as it affected the literature and thought of the period. Rylands told us of the scientists, of the opening up of human knowledge, of Darwin, Lister and Pasteur, of the diverse religious movements through the century, of Cardinal Newman and Keble, of the thoughts of John Stuart Mill and F.W.H.Myers. He traced the position of women to their position during the Great War, from the early days of Mary Wollstonecraft to a most dramatic vignette of Elizabeth Fry in Newgate Jail; Florence Nightingale, the influence of Olive Schreiner; the first women's colleges at Oxford and Cambridge, and finally the suffragettes. We heard about the changing conditions in factories, child labour, the transition from agriculture to industry, and its far-reaching effects upon national life and thought.

Against the rich and fascinating background, G.R. showed us the Brontës at Haworth, Dickens, Thackeray and Jane Austen, Sir Walter Scott, Ouida and Oscar Wilde, closing the century with a study of Thomas Hardy. Rylands presented this grandiose procession of great people as most living, human characters – his inimitable readings from their works were a lesson alone, carefully chosen passages read with drama, irony and humour. Let him but quote Ouida and Oscar Wilde, and we were convulsed with laughter, while G.R. looked serenely solemn ... He recommended books in such a compelling manner that they just had to be read at the first possible moment. ... Those hours spent with Rylands were an exceptional delight ... His lectures opened new fields of thought and reading and interest to me, and my enthusiasm for learning was permanently rekindled.'

Rylands's teaching was not, however, confined to the lecture hall. In his youth he had been an amateur actor, and he believed that the power of great plays could best be conveyed through actual performance. The Marlowe Society had been founded in Cambridge to stage plays by Shakespeare's contemporaries, as well as by Shakespeare himself. From 1928, Rylands became the leading figure in this society, beginning a long series of productions of famous dramas. In so doing he had an influence on the professional theatre in Britain, since many actors, who later became famous, began as students acting in plays produced by Rylands.

But still, it might be objected, Rylands was an academic who was not research active in a society filled with brilliant researchers. Surely he must have been looked down on by those who were more research active. Such an objection confuses the values of Cambridge (Electron to DNA) with those of the contemporary university. The most brilliant researcher at King's College Cambridge in Rylands' day was perhaps Maynard Keynes. Yet Keynes far from looking down on Rylands was one of his great admirers. Indeed Rylands was admired not only by Keynes, but by the whole Bloomsbury group. Should we really be surprised that a literary and artistic coterie were not worried by the fact that Dadie Rylands did not publish many academic papers? Here was a man who had a most profound knowledge of English literature and its history, and who could talk in a brilliant fashion. Is it any wonder that they admired him? Besides Keynes and the Bloomsbury group thought that conveying an appreciation of the culture of the past and present to the next generation was a most important task. Indeed it requires a definite shift in perspective to regard this task as something of secondary importance.

Jones goes as far as to say (2000, p. 4):

'Surely no single figure, not even John Maynard Keynes, his friend and ally, was as omnipresent as Dadie in the twentieth-century history of King's College.'

Another indication of the esteem in which Rylands was held by his colleagues is that fact that when there was a vacancy for the headship of the college in 1956, the majority of the fellows voted for him as the next Provost at the first meeting of the caucuses. However, Rylands decided not to stand for the position. No doubt he preferred study and teaching to administration and management. All this shows that the principle of according high status to teaching in universities is not utopian. This principle was actually embodied in Cambridge (Electron to DNA). A naïve student of Cambridge in that period might conclude that it contained brilliant researchers like Keynes along with 'drop outs' like Rylands who did little or no active research. Such a person might conclude that the system could have been made even more efficient by eliminating the dons like Rylands and retaining only those like Keynes. My thesis to the contrary is that Keynes and Rylands were the two sides of the same coin. The elimination of one would have resulted in the elimination of the other. The high status of teaching in Cambridge (Electron to DNA) was part of the secret of its great success at research.

Chapter 9. A New Role for Peer Reviewing

9.1 Peer Reviewing for Academic Journals

In my sketch in Chapter 8 of a new system for organising non-laboratory research in universities, I gave a role to peer reviewing as part of the promotion process. This might seem odd in the light of my earlier criticisms of peer reviewing. However, my view is not that peer review should be abolished altogether, but rather that it should be given a new role in the overall system of research organisation. At present the principal function of peer reviewing is to select which papers should be published in academic journals. I do indeed think that this should be done away with, both on the grounds of its many defects and because modern technology makes possible a different approach. I will first argue this in detail, and then show that a judicious use of peer reviewing for promotions does not have the defects to be found in the use of peer reviewing for selecting which academic papers to publish in journals.

There seem to me to be three major defects in the use of peer reviewing for the selection of papers to be published in academic journals. The first is that it is likely to lead in many cases to throwing away pink diamonds. I have already dealt at some length with this point and will not repeat my arguments on this subject here. The second defect is that the system is a very costly one. Academic journals are arranged in a hierarchy with the (allegedly) first class most prestigious at the top, then the second class, third class, and so on. Now a typical strategy of an author is to submit his or her paper initially to a first class journal. Here it will be reviewed by 2 or 3 referees. If it is rejected which is the most likely outcome since top journals often have rejection rates of 80-90%, then the author will send it to a second class journal, where again it will be reviewed by 2 or 3 referees. By the time the paper eventually gets published, it may well have been considered by as many as 8 or 9 different referees. It is obvious that a large number of hours of work by referees, editors, and administrative staff of journals will have been carried out in assessing this paper. If we consider the large number of papers being written, and the need that authors have to get them published in order to keep their jobs or gain promotion, we can see that a huge amount of time and effort is involved in the peer review process for selecting papers for journals. A recent article by Zoë Corbyn in the THE (29 May 2008, p. 17) quotes a report by the Cambridge Economic Policy Associates on the cost of peer review. This report "puts the worldwide unpaid cost of peer review at £1.9 billion a year". It might be said of course that since peer reviewing is indeed unpaid, it is not after all a cost to the system. However, this is a naïve reply. If academics did not have to spend so much time on peer reviewing, they would be able to spend more time on teaching and their own research, and so the resources available for teaching and research would increase. The report also says that, regarding the costs per year of research reported in journal articles, they are 'made up of £116 billion for costs of the research itself and £25 billion for publication, distribution and access to the articles.' Thus overall research costs would be considerably reduced if publication, distribution and access could be made cheaper. As we shall see in a moment, modern technology makes possible a reduction in costs in these areas. Let us now turn to the third defect in the current system of selecting articles for publication by peer review. This is that it slows up the process by which articles get into the public domain. Often two or three years may elapse between the date of first submission of an article and its eventual appearance in print. Such long delays in publishing work which may be of great importance are bound to slow up advances in research.

It is not too much to say that the present system of publishing research in peer reviewed academic journals is facing a severe crisis, but help is at hand in the form of the new technology of the internet. Increasingly authors are putting their papers on-line immediately rather than waiting until they appear in a printed journal in two or three years' time. Sometimes they put their papers on their own website, but communal websites are now appearing which put on-line new papers in a particular area before they have been officially published. Actually a paper on-line, provided it is available as open access, is much more convenient than a printed version of the paper in a traditional journal. To read the printed version, a trip to the library is necessary, and the researcher has to spend time there to read the paper, or perhaps will need to make a photocopy of the paper to take away. If the paper is available on-line and open access, the researcher can download it at his or her own computer, and print a copy if necessary. Thus a new system is coming into existence before our eyes, and my suggestion is that it should entirely replace the present system of peer reviewed academic journals. Papers can simply be put on-line and open access without any peer reviewing, leaving the research community to make what they like of them.

9.2 Objections to an Open Access System without Peer Review

Let us now consider what objections might be made to such a system. The obvious one is that it would result in the entry to the public domain of an enormous quantity of rubbish. So much rubbish would appear that researchers would be quite unable to find the needle of a good paper in the midst of this haystack of valueless material. 'Surely', it could be argued, 'we must have some quality control over what appears, or researchers will have no guide as to what is good, and the system will collapse in a superfluity of rubbish. The peer reviewing system, whatever its defects, does provide at least some element of quality control.' This could be called: 'the needle in the haystack argument'. I will return to it in a moment, but first let us consider a particular aspect of this argument, which might be termed: 'the crank objection'.

The crank objection is that, without the control exercised by peer reviewing, a huge torrent of publications by cranks would be unleashed. But who is a crank? I will now attempt a description of a crank, and will assume that our hypothetical crank is male, since, for some reason, most cranks do seem to be male. Our typical crank starts life as a not very good student who skips lectures and prefers to read on his own rather than listening to his experienced teachers. In fact he probably holds eminent professors in contempt. Not surprisingly he ends up with very mediocre grades on his degree. He may go on to try for a PhD, but will certainly fail to get that. He gets bad references from the eminent professors he scorned, and is more or less drummed out of the academic world. Nonetheless, such is the strength of the 'crank spirit' that our crank continues to believe that he has really good ideas on the subject which he failed to study with any attention. While occupied in a humdrum job, he writes reams of papers putting forward weird crankish ideas. 'Luckily', a defender of the present system might say, 'these effusions do not appear because they are rejected by the peer reviewing system. Abolish peer review and floods of these crank productions will appear.'

Now there undoubtedly is a crank community which exists on the fringes of academe. Yet it is dangerous to be too hard on this community, because, every so often, one of their members turns out to be right when the mainstream community is wrong. In fact the description of the 'crank' in the previous paragraph was designed to be an exact fit to Einstein in 1905, and Einstein in 1905 published his paper on Special Relativity which has become the most famous scientific paper of the 20th century. I will now briefly describe Einstein's life up to 1905.[8]

9.3 Einstein's Life up to 1905

Einstein was born on 14 March 1879, and entered the Swiss Polytechnic Institute in Zurich in October 1896, aged 17. He graduated in July 1900, aged 21. However his grades were not outstanding. Of the five candidates who graduated on his course, Einstein was placed fourth (Miller, 2001, p. 67). Einstein had been far from a model student, at least from his teachers' point of view. He had skipped lectures regularly, and preferred to study the masters of theoretical physics on his own. For the exams, he relied on the notes taken by his friend Marcel Grossmann. Einstein hoped that Professor Heinrich

Friedrich Weber, a distinguished contemporary physicist, might take him on in the paid position of assistant. However, Weber appointed two mechanical engineering students instead. In fairness to Weber, Einstein's grades had not been very good, but there may have been tensions between him and Einstein on the personal level. Einstein apparently regularly addressed Weber as 'Herr Weber' rather than 'Herr Professor Weber' (Miller, 2001, p. 52). This was obviously a serious failing in a German-speaking university of that time.

Despite failing to get an assistantship, Einstein enrolled to do a PhD with Weber, but things did not work out, and Einstein left Weber's laboratory in the spring of 1901. He now tried offering his services as an assistant to other professors, but with no success. Einstein blamed his failure on bad references from Weber. On 27 March 1901, he wrote to his partner Mileva (quoted from Miller, 2001, p. 280):

'I'm absolutely convinced that Weber is to blame ... I'm convinced that under these circumstances it doesn't make any sense to write to any more professors, because they'll surely turn to Weber for information about me at a certain point, and he'll just give me another bad recommendation.'

This analysis sounds correct. Perhaps Einstein had realised too late that it was dangerous to be disrespectful to Herr Professors. It must be remembered that his acts of disrespect and partial rebellion took place mainly when he was still a teenager. Now in his early twenties, he was suffering the consequences. Moreover worse was to follow.

After his break with Herr Professor Weber, Einstein decided to submit his PhD thesis not to the Swiss Polytechnic Institute at Zurich, but to the University of Zurich. However in February 1902, the thesis was rejected because of Einstein's sharp criticisms of Boltzmann's theory of gases (Miller, 2001, p. 70). Einstein's hopes of getting a paid position in a university had so far come to nothing, and in June 1902, he started work at the Swiss Federal Patent Office in Bern.

After these experiences, most people would have given up all hopes of becoming a research scientist, but not Einstein. He remained convinced of his own abilities at theoretical physics. In Bern, he formed a small discussion group with a few friends. They called themselves the Olympia Academy, and met regularly to discuss philosophy and theoretical physics between 1902 and 1904. Einstein devoted his free time to writing papers on theoretical physics which he managed to get published in the leading German journal of physics, the *Annalen der Physik* . These published papers included his famous 1905 paper which introduced the Special Theory of Relativity.

I can now return to the question which I raised earlier (**4.3**) of how Einstein managed to get his 1905 paper published. This paper not only introduces a radically new approach, but does not cite any other paper or book on the subject. These features according to my earlier analysis make it the type of paper most likely to be rejected by peer review. Arthur I. Miller agrees with this judgement, writing (2001, p. 191):

'Today no leading physics journal would publish it because of its complete lack of citations to the literature.'

Miller provides the answer to this question by explaining the editorial policy of the *Annalen der Physik* (2001, p. 193):

'The *Annalen*'s editorial policy was that an author's initial publications were scrutinized either by the editor or a member of the Curatorium. Subsequent papers were published without further refereeing.'

In the years 1901-4, Einstein had published 5 papers in the *Annalen der Physik* – 1 in 1901, 2 in 1902, 1 in 1903, and 1 in 1904. Some of these papers would have been subjected to a process of scrutiny similar to peer review. However, by 1905 he was an established author for the *Annalen*, and in the normal course of events, his paper would have been accepted for publication without any peer review. Another circumstance which favoured Einstein (cf. Miller, 2001, p. 191) was that the *Annalen* did not give an author's academic affiliation, but just the city from which the paper had been sent. Thus Einstein's ends his paper with 'Bern, June 1905'. So most readers would have assumed that the author was at the University of Bern, and would not have realised that he had no university post.

It is interesting to note here that Einstein's early papers for the *Annalen* were less revolutionary, and more mainstream than some of his papers of 1905. In a letter of 1907, Einstein describes the first two of his *Annalen* papers as 'my two worthless first papers' (quoted from Miller, 2001, p. 71). Arthur I. Miller considers that here Einstein is being unduly self-critical. The truth is probably that the first papers were sound but not very inspiring – just the sort of papers that get accepted by peer review. Of course Einstein may not yet have arrived at his radical new ideas, but another possibility is that, after his rather bitter experiences with Herr Professor Weber, he had realised that less radical work was more likely to get accepted. He may then have been following the deliberate strategy of getting himself established with less striking papers, and then, when he was to some extent established, launching his revolutionary ideas. Evidence that Einstein may have adopted such a plan is provided by his second and successful attempt to get a PhD. In 1905 he published 3 papers in the *Annalen der Physik*. The first was on quantum theory and the third is the Special Relativity paper. These two are central to the revolution in physics which started that year. However, when Einstein made his second attempt to obtain a PhD from the University of Zurich, his thesis: 'On a New Determination of Molecular Dimensions' was based on the second *Annalen* paper (Miller, 2001, p. 190). This second paper is of course brilliant, but it is perhaps less revolutionary than the other two. This does suggest that Einstein had learnt from his earlier negative experiences to tread warily in academic matters.

9.4 A Suggested Revival of the Editorial Policies of the Annalen der Physik

Let us now turn from the particular example of Einstein to the general policy regarding the publication of academic papers which prevailed in his day. It must come as a great surprise that a leading academic journal such as the *Annalen der Physik* would automatically accept papers from any established author without any refereeing procedure. How different this is from today! Obviously at that time there were relatively few researchers in physics and so the *Annalen* could adopt such a policy without creating any undue pressure on space. As the number of researchers grew, the need to keep the size of the journal within reasonable limits would have prevented such a policy being continued, and it is probable that, at this stage, the system of peer review was introduced to select those papers worthy of publication. Now, however, with the new technology of the internet and on-line publication, constraints of space disappear, since there is an indefinitely large amount of room in cyber-space for papers. Thus the old system of the *Annalen der Physik*, which worked so well at the beginning of the 20th century, can be reintroduced at the beginning of the 21st century. Academic journals can now all become electronic and open access. Authors who are beginning their career would have to prove their worth by having a PhD and/or having their first couple of papers peer reviewed, but, once they have established themselves in this way, they would be free to publish any further papers in the journal with no further refereeing and only a minimum of vetting by the editor. This system would overcome all the defects we noted in the system of peer reviewed printed journals. The new system would be much less costly. Not only would it save the burden of peer reviewing, but it would considerably reduce the costs of printing and distribution. Papers would appear immediately instead of with a delay of two or three years, and so advances in research would be speeded up. Finally almost no pink diamonds would be thrown away. Authors who were capable of at least starting in a reasonably mainstream way at the stage of their PhD and early papers, could thereafter be as revolutionary as they wished, in the manner of Einstein, and still get their papers into the public domain.

9.5 The Needle in the Haystack Objection

This new system of publication, far from being utopian, is actually coming into existence spontaneously. Yet there are bound to be defenders of the older system of peer reviewed printed journals. So it would be as well to consider what objections to the new system they might raise. The principal objection would I think be the objection already mentioned which I described as the needle in the haystack objection. The number of researchers is already very large and is likely to continue to increase. If all these researchers are allowed, with few checks, to put their papers into the public domain, everyone attempting research will find themselves facing a huge mountain of literature, most of which will almost certainly be of little importance. How are researchers then to find the needle of a good paper among the haystack of papers in cyber-space? There is indeed a problem here, and it exists already under the present system, since the system of peer reviewing is at present producing quite a haystack of papers. However, there are ways in which this problem can be tackled, and I will now describe a very hopeful approach which has been set out by Grazia Ietto-Gillies in her 2008.

9.6 Peer Comment instead of Peer Review

Ietto-Gillies advocates on-line publication without peer review, but she suggests that, instead of peer review, there should be a system of what she calls: **Peer Comment**. She describes this as follows (2008, p. 18):

'For each paper published on Open Access the editor should open an electronic "Comments Link" inviting readers to send comments which ... will then be placed on the Link site. These open debates should be positively encouraged as a way of developing research; they are a way of recognizing that research is a social activity and the interaction of various researchers can aid progress.'

Of course peer comment differs very radically from peer review. Ietto-Gillies lists some of the differences as follows (2008, p. 18):

'(a) it is based on a potentially much larger number of commentators; (b) it is not power-based in the sense that the commentators do not have the power to stop the paper being put into the public domain: it is already there; and (c) the comments are signed unlike the anonymous referees' reports.'

One objection which might be made is that since comments are open and signed, commentators might not be so critical as they would be if the comments were anonymous. However, experience of academe strongly suggests that this is not a serious problem. For the most part, academics really love attacking those who hold different opinions, and editors who monitor these open debates may have to urge commentators to remove rude and offensive remarks.

One point in favour of peer comment as opposed to peer review is that it would not impose such a burden on researchers. Very often researchers are called upon to referee a paper which is on a topic which is not part of their current research. Maybe it is something on which they worked in the past, and with which they have now got bored. To be forced to read a paper in these circumstances is a tedious effort, which encourages a hasty perusal of the paper, and perhaps, as a result, a not very carefully considered judgement on it. Peer comment would, by contrast, be entirely voluntary. Researchers would only choose to comment on a paper if it was directly related to research which they were actively pursuing. They would therefore approach the task with energy and enthusiasm, and produce more carefully thought out comments. The work would be a part of their current research, not a forced interruption of that research.

Give a system of peer comment, some papers will attract vigorous comments while others will be ignored, and this at once gives some guidance to researchers as to which papers might be worth looking at. However, Ietto-Gillies suggests some further ways in which the needle in the haystack problem might be overcome. She writes (2008, p. 19):

'The publication of articles on "Literature Surveys" should be encouraged in order to help readers sift through the large amount of literature now available. In fact doctoral students world wide engage in this useful activity; papers from this part of their effort are usually not published; we should encourage their publication because it may provide a useful feed back for authors and other interested researchers. It could be argued that good literature reviews are not easy and they need considerably more experience than that of the average research student. I tend to agree with this and I suggest that experienced people should also get involved in this.'

These considerations lead to a further criticism of the RAE. The writing of 'literature surveys' is a very useful activity for the community, but few researchers in the UK now do it because such literature surveys do not count towards the RAE. Ietto-Gillies makes this point as regards reviews in general (2008, p. 19):

'Reviews of web articles as well as of books should be encouraged as they perform a very valuable service; this would reverse a trend of the last couple of decades which have seen the downgrading of book reviews for the purpose of the RAE or jobs and grants applications. This downgrading discourages authors from employing their time in reviewing activities and deprives the community of a useful tool for selection and discrimination of which papers/books to read.'

We see then that the needle in the haystack problem can be solved through a combination of peer comment, and the encouragement of reviews and literature surveys. Peer review does not solve this problem so satisfactorily, while, characteristically, the RAE puts obstacles in the way of its solution.

9.7 Will the Open Access/Peer Comment System in fact increase the Size of the Haystack?

If the barrier of peer review is removed, it would seem that more papers will appear in the public domain. This would increase the size of the haystack and make looking for the needles which it contains more difficult. But is it really the case that the open access/peer comment system will increase the size of the haystack? I will now argue that if the open access/peer comment system is introduced together with the new system of research organisation sketched in Chapter 8, then the size of the haystack is likely to decrease rather than increase.

Under the present system of research organisation, nearly all academics have to publish a number of articles in peer reviewed journals or they will be subjected to heavy penalties and perhaps even lose their jobs. This means that an academic who has run out of research ideas, and perhaps is not very good at research or interested in it, must perforce write research papers and get them published. This 'publish or perish' feature of the present system of course results in the appearance of a whole mass of papers which may be competent enough, but do not contain any new material of great interest. In other words it produces an increase in the size of the haystack. Now in the system suggested in Chapter 8, this pressure to publish would disappear. Those academics who had decided to specialise in teaching might not publish anything at all, and use their research time for study research rather than active research. As we saw from the case of George Rylands (**8.9**), this happened in Cambridge (Electron to DNA). Similarly those who had decided to specialise in admin might not publish anything. Even those who were climbing the research ladder would only need to publish if they wanted to try for a promotion. Without the pressure to publish, researchers would only put their ideas into the public domain if they thought that they had something important to say. Thus the new system would tend to diminish the size of the haystack and increase the number of needles in it.

One important principle emerges from this. There is no point in trying to force researchers who are reluctant to publish to do so. Indeed this practice is harmful. Research papers are only likely to be good if they are produced by enthusiastic researchers. Researchers who have run out of ideas and do not want to publish will almost certainly produce bad papers if they are forced to publish in order to keep their jobs. Thus the net effect of the 'publish or perish' principle is to increase the size of the haystack without increasing the number of needles in it. I will explore some consequences of this principle in Chapter 11.

It should also be remembered that the open access/peer comment system is not without quality controls. To begin with, a researcher has to gain the right to enter a particular on-line journal either by having a PhD in the subject or by having two or three papers peer reviewed in the traditional manner. This limits contributors to well-qualified people, and eliminates the complete cranks without stifling the highly innovative thinkers. Secondly open peer comment can be quite a mortifying experience for authors who make mistakes. As already pointed out, many academics greatly enjoy pointing out the faults and errors of others. Thus an author who publishes a foolish piece of work is likely to have his or her mistakes exposed in a very public manner. Peer reviews may be wounding, but at least they are anonymous. So the system of open comment would act as a considerable disincentive for authors to publish ill-considered papers. This again would tend to diminish the size of the haystack.

On a more positive note, the system of open peer comment is a powerful tool for eliminating errors and improving papers. This point is made as follows by Numerico and Bowen (2007, p.2):

'Wikipedians and the other open science initiatives participants are more capable of a dynamic reaction in comparison to what the established science process can guarantee. If there is some mistake in the Wikipedia entries, it is very easily and quickly corrected by another expert in the field. This efficient performance cannot be assured within a more traditional encyclopedia production system, such as the Encyclopedia Britannica, for example, whose peer reviewed entries are less controlled and less easily corrected, being part of a more hierarchical enterprise, as it was proved from an experimental comparison between the two.'

9.8 The Use of Peer Review in Appointments and Promotions

On-line publication and open debates in cyber-space are currently becoming a standard part of the research scene. Yet the traditional peer reviewed printed journals are continuing. Why is this? The answer is that such journals are used as the basis for assessment for appointments and promotions. Typically a researcher nowadays will put his or her new paper on-line immediately, but still go through the tedious task of getting it published in a journal of as high a grade as possible. Other researchers will make use of the paper as soon as it appears on-line. By the time the paper finally appears in print in a peer reviewed journal in two or three years' time, the research community may have moved on. However, the appearance of the paper is important for its author because it constitutes the basis of attempts to obtain an appointment or promotion. Thus the production and distribution of all those peer reviewed printed academic journals at enormous cost (c. £25 billion per annum) is only really now justified as a part of an assessment system. Surely it would be sensible to introduce a much cheaper and simpler assessment system rather than continuing with this unnecessary expense. I will now sketch such a simpler and cheaper assessment system for appointments and promotions. It is based on peer review, and I will also show that peer review does not in this context have the defects which it has in the present system.

Let us begin with the case of a researcher who obtains an academic job, and decides to opt for the research ladder. After some years (let us say 10), he or she decides to apply for a promotion from the lowest grade (in the UK, lecturer) to the next higher grade (in the UK, senior lecturer). How can the college's promotion committee assess the value of this candidate's research? The obvious scheme would be something along these lines. The candidate has to write a short account of the research he or she has carried out during the preceding ten years, and to submit it with what he or she judges to be his or her best 4 published pieces of work (books or papers). The committee then selects 3 referees working in the candidate's field, and sends each of them copies of the candidate's work for comment. The decision on whether to promote the candidate is made largely on the basis of the reports of these referees. A similar procedure could be followed for appointments, except that, in this case, the members of the appointing department could act as the referees who judge the candidate's work. Such a system is clearly simple and straightforward to operate. It remains to show that the peer reviewing which it involves does not have the defects of peer reviewing in the present system.

We noted above three defects in peer reviewing in the present system. The first defect was that it could lead to throwing away pink diamonds. Now it is still possible that a pink diamond might, under the new system proposed, be refused promotion for reasons which in retrospect appear unfair. This actually happened to Frege who never reached the highest grade of full professor in the University of Jena. No doubt there will be future Freges who experience a similar fate. However, in the new system proposed, the maltreatment of pink diamonds will not have such serious consequences as it does under the present RAE system. Under the present system a rejected pink diamond may be unable to publish his or her work, and may have his or her research time cut. In the new system, the rejected pink diamond will be able to publish his or her work, and to continue with the same amount of research time. Their only misfortune will be a failure to obtain promotion. This is certainly a very considerable improvement. Moreover there is a further consideration which makes errors of peer review less likely under the new system. If a peer reviewer receives out of the blue a paper which seems to adopt a strange and seemingly crankish approach, his or her first reaction is very likely to be that this is nonsense and not worth publishing. Under the new system however, the same peer reviewer would receive an explanation from the author about his or her new approach and how it has been followed over a number of years. Having read this explanation, and then been able to peruse four examples of the research resulting from the new approach, the peer reviewer is more likely to be able to gain a better understanding of this new approach, and so perhaps to judge it more fairly. In fact applying for a promotion may in the future be a way in which hitherto undiscovered pink diamonds may finally make the breakthrough of getting their work better known and understood.

The second defect of contemporary peer reviewing is that it is very costly. However, if peer reviewing is limited to assessments for appointments and promotions, the amount of peer reviewing needed will be drastically reduced, and it will no longer be a burdensome cost on the system.

The third defect of contemporary peer reviewing is that is introduces a long delay between the completion of a paper and its finally appearing in print in a peer reviewed journal. Obviously this is no longer a defect in the present system, since papers are published electronically without peer review, and peer review is used only for assessments for appointments and promotions.

Apart from these principal defects, there are some other defects of the peer review system as it exists at present which are also avoided by the new use for peer reviewing here suggested. One such additional defect, which was noted earlier (**4.3** and **6.2**), concerns the tendency for authors to introduce citations and flattering comments just to get their papers published. If an author is submitting a paper to a journal, it is often quite easy to guess who the referees are likely to be. The author has only to look through the back numbers of the journal, and see what academics have been publishing papers there in his field. The editor is quite likely to choose some of these academics as referees. So our hopeful author may increase the chance of getting his or her paper published by citing these academics, praising their work, and claiming that his or her own paper is a development of their ideas, even though he or she thinks their papers are rubbish, and these papers had not the slightest influence on his or her thinking. As I pointed out earlier (**6.2**), bogus citations of this kind are very harmful to the academic enterprise. For example they may recommend the reader to study papers which the author really thinks are valueless. This makes the needle in the haystack problem harder to solve. Moreover by giving the reader a false account of how the author arrived at his or her ideas, these bogus citations may hinder the understanding of these ideas. One big objection to the use of metrics for evaluation purposes is that this will amplify this problem through the formation of citation clubs. The use of peer review for appointments and promotions in the manner described above will not encourage bogus citations, however. An author will be able to publish his or her paper on-line without any peer reviewing. The paper may in 5 or 10 years' time form part of a package which goes to some anonymous referees for peer review. However, at the time of writing it will be impossible to guess who these peer reviewers will be, or even whether the paper itself will form part of some future 'promotion package' put together by the author. Thus there is no incentive for the author to make bogus citations. There is, however, still an incentive for the author to avoid plagiarism since plagiarism can, and surely would be, easily exposed by the peer comment system. Authors whose work is plagiarised are very likely to draw this to the attention of the research community.

To sum up then, the proposal is not to abolish peer reviewing altogether but to give it a new role. In this new role, peer reviewing no longer has the defects which arise out of its use in the present system.

Chapter 10. Improving Administration and Management: (i) Analysis of an Example

10.1 Double Worsening

We have seen that measures designed to improve teaching can have the indirect effect of improving research. The same is true of administration and management or 'admin' for short. As I will show in this section, measures designed to improve admin can have the indirect effect of improving research. Most academics carry out three types of activity – research, teaching and admin. My general idea is that by taking measures to improve the second and third of these activities, we will succeed in improving the first.

But what exactly constitutes an improvement in admin? Here account must be taken of a fundamental difference between admin on the one hand, and teaching and research on the other. Teaching and research are the productive activities of the university whose purpose is to generate new knowledge (research) and to transmit old and new knowledge (teaching). It is not the purpose of the university to carry out admin. That is not to say that admin is unnecessary. On the contrary, though unproductive in itself, it is essential, since a large organisation simply could not function without admin. However, though essential, it is desirable that it is kept to the minimum necessary. If the same result can be achieved with less admin, then this is preferable to having more admin. In other words, admin is improved if the number of hours devoted to admin is reduced. This is in obvious contrast to teaching and research. These are activities which, generally speaking, are improved by having more hours devoted to them.

Now, unfortunately, as far as research is concerned, the past few decades have seen a very large increase in the amount of admin required of the researcher. This of course increases the cost of research as can be seen by a simple example. Suppose that a researcher originally spent 10% of his or her time on admin. Then, due to a change in regulations, he or she has to spend 20% of his or her time on admin. If we assume that salaries have remained the same, then the amount of money which would previously buy 90 units of research time, will now buy only 80 units of research time. In other words, the cost of a unit of research time has increased by 12.5%. This gives an idea of the additional funding costs incurred by imposing administrative burdens on researchers.

Now it could be that although the cost of a unit of research time has increased because of the new regulations, the overall output of research increases both in quality and quantity, so that the efficiency of the system improves. Unfortunately this is not at all the case. The new regulations have in all cases led not only to an increase in the costs of research time, but also to a decline in the quality of the research output. Thus, there has been a **double worsening** of the situation as regards research. Its costs have risen while the quality of the output has declined. Naturally this situation is not the fault of the researchers, but of the governments who have imposed on researchers a series of new regulations, bureaucratic controls, etc. which have made the system as a whole function worse than it did before.

The RAE which we discussed in Part 1 of the book is a perfect example of this negative development, because, as we have seen, it increases the costs of research, while diminishing the quality of research output. However, the RAE is not the only example of this trend, and similar negative developments can be seen in most aspects of research organisation. I will now illustrate this by analysing one example in detail. The example is, in itself, a very small part of overall research organisation in the UK. Yet it is representative of the negative developments which have occurred everywhere in the last two or three decades, and so is well worth careful consideration.

10.2 AHRB (2001)

The example concerns a particular research leave scheme designed for researchers in the humanities. The first version of this scheme (henceforth, the old scheme) was run by the British Academy for a number of years up till the late 1990s. The old scheme was quite sensible in character, and had rather low administrative costs. If a researcher in the humanities could obtain a term of research leave from his or her university, he or she could then apply to the British Academy for a further term of research leave. If successful, the British Academy would pay the researcher's university the cost of replacement teaching and admin, leaving the researcher with a further term free to devote to research. After the end of the research leave, the researcher had to write a short report on what he or she had done. The researcher was also required to send any papers or books produced in the period of research leave to the British Academy, with the financial help of the British Academy duly acknowledged. Since publication can require two or three years, the British Academy allowed a similar period of time for the papers or books to arrive. In fact the British Academy has a considerable collection of papers and books which are testimony to the success of the old scheme.

One might have thought that such a straightforward and successful scheme would have been allowed to continue, but not so. In some circles it was obviously thought that this scheme was old-fashioned and needed to be modernised for the twenty-first century. I will next describe the new scheme as it was formulated in September 2001, and then show that the effects of the new regulations were a typical double worsening relative to the old scheme.

The old scheme was run by the British Academy, but the running of the new scheme was taken over by what was called the Arts and Humanities Research Board (AHRB). In September 2001, the AHRB issued a Guide to the Research Leave Scheme [henceforth AHRB (2001)]. This guide explains the details of the new scheme in a document of 28 pages. It has to be said that such bureaucratic documents do not in general make very enjoyable reading. However, I will try to show that the judicious mind can find much of interest in the pages of AHRB (2001).

In the introduction the authors of AHRB (2001) explain that (p. 5): 'From April 2001, the Board became a company ... . The new corporate status will allow the AHRB to continue to develop a more independent and distinctive identity and to have a more direct relationship with the community it serves.' This remark is very typical of that historical period in the UK. 2001, two years before the beginning of the Iraq war, was perhaps the high point of Blair's ascendancy. At that time, corporations, such as banks or supermarkets, were seen as the model which government organisations should follow in order to serve the community better. AHRB (2001) begins on p. 2 with a **MISSION STATEMENT**, and a list of **Strategic priorities**. In so doing the document models itself on the annual reports of companies which often began in the same way at that time. A portion of the AHRB's mission statement runs as follows (p. 2): 'The AHRB's mission is to: promote and support excellence in research in the arts and humanities ... to enhance the quality of life and creative output of the nation.' These are noble ideals, but the question of expense is not forgotten, for one of the strategic priorities is (p.2): '*securing value*: to promote the best possible use of public funds by ensuring value for money and demonstrable value in all the Board's programmes and activities.' Alas, neither the noble ideals nor the value for money were achieved. As I will show the changes introduced by the AHRB resulted in an increase in the cost of research with a reduction in the quality of the research output – a typical double worsening.

But what were the changes introduced into the new scheme for research leave? First of all the application procedure became much more complicated. At the end of AHRB (2001), there is a copy of the application form with a further 3 pages of guidance notes on how to fill it in. The heart of the application is of course the description of the research which the candidate wants to carry out. However, the candidate is certainly not allowed to use his or her initiative in describing the research. The description must be given in terms of a scheme devised by the AHRB. The relevant section begins: '**You should read the guidance notes provided before completing this section.**', and the applicant is then told to use the following sub-headings:

' • Research question(s)
• Aims and objectives
• Research context
• Research methods
• Timetable for completion within the period of leave (please refer to guidance notes for definition of completion)
• Plans for public dissemination (eg. publication, exhibition, performance)'

Of course the applicant might very well think that the scheme devised by the AHRB is not an appropriate one for describing his or her research, but then 'rules are rules'. Moreover the instructions conclude with the following instruction: 'Please complete the word-count box provided: if you exceed the word limit, your application will be deemed ineligible for funding and will be returned to you.'

Filling in an application form is, however, only the beginning. The candidate has to find two external assessors who are then sent a complicated form with guidelines about how to fill it in. They have to use this form to give an assessment of the candidate's application. After that (AHRB, 2001, p. 13): 'The external assessors' reports together with your application form will be sent for assessment to peer reviewers...', because, as we would expect, (AHRB, 2001, p. 12): 'The Board is committed to the principle of peer review in its Advanced Research competitions.'

So far the AHRB has introduced quite a lot of extra complexity into the application procedure. However, the most striking innovation of the AHRB is not here, but rather in what happens after the completion of the period of research leave. This is described in the sections of AHRB (2001) dealing with monitoring, and we will now give a brief account of the new procedures introduced.

Addressing the candidate, AHRB (2001) says (p.19):

'You must submit an end-of-award report within three months of the end of the period covered by the award. ... In the report you will be asked to provide a self-assessment of the extent to which you have met the original aims and objectives of the research, ... The report will normally be assessed through peer review.'

The more detailed instructions require that the scheme of research from the original application be attached to the end-of-award report and referred to when completing the end-of-award report. The end-of-award report with its attachment is then sent for peer review so that the peer reviewers can judge to what extent the original plan has been carried out.

Two points can be made immediately about this. First of all it introduces a new round of peer review after the completion of the research leave. This did not exist in the old scheme, and so represents an increase in the general burden of administration on the research community, thereby driving up the costs of research. Secondly, and more strikingly, the AHRB are imposing a particular strategy for carrying out research. This strategy has two parts. (1) A detailed plan for future research must be drawn up. This plan must use categories imposed by the AHRB, and not categories selected by the researcher himself or herself. (2) This plan must be strictly adhered to. We can summarise this strategy as that of strict adherence to earlier detailed research plans.

The AHRB make clear that they fully endorse this strategy of strict adherence when they go on to describe how the peer reviewers will be required to assess the end-of-award report, and also the penalties which will fall on the heads of those researchers who have bad end-of-award reports. The peer reviewers are required to assess the end-of-award report using the following three categories: satisfactory, problematic, and unsatisfactory. The authors of AHRB (2001) go on to say (p.20):

'*unsatisfactory* – indicates a project that ... has failed to conduct the research as agreed at the time of the award (and any subsequent agreed changes to the plan of research), and which therefore does not meet the regulations and the aims and objectives of the particular scheme of awards.'

They then list the penalties to which the unfortunate researcher who has an unsatisfactory end-of-award report will be subjected. A selection from these penalties runs as follows (p. 20):

'If your end-of-award report is assessed as unsatisfactory:
    • we will write to you, and to your host institution, to inform you of the status of the report.
    • you will be debarred from making applications to any of the AHRB's research schemes for two years, ... We will write to you, and to the Head of your institution, confirming the penalty
    ...
    • we will keep a record of the unsatisfactory assessment on file, and this will be taken into consideration when you make further applications to the AHRB.'

These penalties are very harsh – particularly for a young researcher. Such a researcher, on receiving an unsatisfactory assessment, is debarred from applying for any research funding from the AHRB for two years, and, since the unsatisfactory report will be kept on file, it becomes very unlikely that he or she will get any further research funding from the AHRB even after two years. As the AHRB is one of the few sources for research funding in the humanities, this is a heavy blow to the young researcher's hopes of a research career. In addition, there will be a letter to the Head of the researcher's institution confirming the penalty, and this makes it unlikely that the unfortunate researcher will get further research leave from that institution, as well as damaging promotion prospects. The curious thing about these heavy penalties is that they are quite compatible with the researcher having worked hard during the period of research leave, and even with the researcher having done what is generally agreed to be brilliant research. This is because one of the criteria for getting an unsatisfactory assessment is explicitly stated to be failure 'to conduct the research as agreed at the time of the award.'

That concludes my account of the new system introduced by the AHRB in September 2001. I will now show that it represents a double worsening relative to the old scheme which the British Academy had operated previously. The first part of the worsening is obvious. The new scheme imposes a heavier administrative burden both on the candidate and the research community, thereby driving up the cost of research. As far as the candidate is concerned, there are much more complicated forms to be filled in, both when applying and after the period of research leave is completed. I would estimate that at least a week's work would be required for this, and as the grant is only for 10 weeks' research leave, the effective research leave is reduced by a week to 9 weeks. From the point of view of the funding body, this represents an increase of 11% in the cost of the research time granted. However administrative burdens are also imposed on the two external assessors who have to fill in complicated forms, and on further peer reviewers. Indeed, as we have seen, the new system introduces a further round of peer reviewing which did not exist in the old system. To keep matters in perspective, it is worth considering the size of the grant in relation to the standards of government expenditure. The grant offers research leave for a period of one term, i.e. ten weeks. This is slightly less than 20% of an annual salary. However the academic who obtains the award might well have research time amounting to about 25% of his or her time, with the remaining 75% devoted to teaching and admin. Thus the amount of the grant would be a bit less than 15% of an academic's annual salary. Moreover academics are, relative to their qualifications, a very badly paid group. The average academic earns only about a third of the salary of a G.P. Thus, on this estimate, the amount of the grant on this research leave scheme is rather less than 5% of the annual salary of a typical G.P. Of course, this estimate is a bit crude. Still, if we estimate the value of a research leave grant at between 5 and 10% of a G.P.'s salary, we cannot be too far out. For a sum of this magnitude is it really worth setting up such an elaborate and time-consuming system for applying and monitoring? There really seems to be a complete lack of common sense in so doing.

It can hardly be denied then, that the new scheme of the AHRB increases the cost of research. However, it could be said in defence of the AHRB that this increase in costs is likely to be more than compensated for by an increase in the quality of the research produced because of the new monitoring procedures introduced. We will now show that far from increasing the quality of the research produced, the new scheme is likely to make it worse. This will then establish the claimed double worsening.

10.3 First Example: Fleming's Discovery of Penicllin

The key innovation of the new scheme was, as we have seen, to impose on researchers the strategy of strict adherence to earlier detailed research plans. Is this a good strategy for carrying out research? It does not require a great deal of reflection to see that it is a very bad plan. In fact, even a superficial study of the history of science, the history of philosophy etc. shows that the biggest advances in research occur precisely when the researcher gives up an earlier plan and pursues a new course. The change of direction may occur because a chance observation, or a new idea, suddenly makes the researcher see that his or her old plan of research is likely to lead nowhere, and, at the same time, offers the possibility of a much more fruitful direction for the research to take. An exciting new path has opened up before the researcher, and by following this path, he or she is led to new and important advances in the field. The AHRB, however, imposes heavy penalties on any researcher who acts in this way, and this is why the new scheme is likely to reduce the quality of the research produced. Just how serious this reduction might be can be seen by considering some examples of big advances which were produced when researchers changed their earlier plans. I will now briefly discuss two such examples.

The first example concerns one of the most notable discoveries in the entire history of medicine, namely Fleming's discovery of penicillin. The following is a very brief sketch of how this occurred.[9] Fleming made his discovery when engaged in a piece of fairly routine research into the staphylococcus bacterium. Staphylococci are responsible for a variety of infectious diseases – some quite serious. The most virulent form of the bacterium is the golden coloured staphylococcus aureus. There are also staphylococci with other colours, e.g. white, which are much less virulent. In 1927 or 1928, Fleming read a paper claiming that colonies of staphylococci changed colour if they were kept at room temperature for several days. If true, this would mean that the staphylococci might lose their virulence, a suggestion which was in line with a well-known principle introduced by Pasteur in the 19th century, that of *oxygen attenuation*. Pasteur discovered that many pathogenic bacteria lose some of their virulence if exposed to oxygen for lengthy periods. The bacteria might in some cases be treated with oxygen gas, but in others a simple exposure to air for a protracted period could suffice. Pasteur used this principle to create vaccines.

Perhaps because of its connection with Pasteur's principle, Fleming decided to check the claims of the paper he had read by conducting a programme to investigate colour changes in staphylococci. His procedure was very simple. He prepared colonies of staphylococci in Petri dishes, and left these dishes on his bench, examining them every few days to see if changes in the colour of some of the staphylococci could be observed. This is a typical instance of what Kuhn would call normal science. If successful, the research might establish another instance of Pasteur's well-known principle of oxygen attenuation.

Fleming began this research with the help of an assistant called Pryce, who, however, left the laboratory in February 1928 to start another job. Fleming continued the work on his own throughout the summer, and, at the end of July, went off for this usual summer holiday, leaving a number of culture-plates piled at the end of his bench where they would be out of the sunlight. Early in September (probably on 3 September), when Fleming had returned from his holiday, Pryce dropped in to see him. Fleming was sorting out the pile of Petri dishes on his bench. He selected a few of these to show to Pryce, including one which he had already discarded because it was contaminated. As he looked at this plate with Pryce, Fleming suddenly said: 'That's funny'.

The plate in question had become contaminated with a green mould. This was a common enough occurrence in bacteriological experiments, and generally meant that the plate was of no further use for the research being carried out, and would need to be discarded. When Fleming looked again at this plate, however, he noticed, as he explained in his paper of 1929, that the staphylococcus colonies, which would normally cover the whole plate, had become transparent or disappeared altogether in the area near the mould. This suggested to Fleming that the mould might be producing a substance capable of destroying dangerous pathogenic bacteria, and hence potentially of great use in medicine. The mould was later identified as *penicillium notatum*, and Fleming gave the name 'penicillin' to the anti-bacterial substance which he thought, correctly as it turned out, the mould might be producing.

What is relevant to our consideration of AHRB (2001) is that Fleming, immediately after making the crucial observation of the contaminated plate, abandoned completely the research on which he was engaged, and started working on a completely different research programme designed to investigate the properties of penicillin. Now let us suppose that Fleming's earlier research on colour change in staphylococci had been funded by a scheme modelled on AHRB (2001). Fleming would have earlier submitted a proposal detailing his plan to investigate colour changes in staphylococci. As this was a sensible piece of normal science, it would probably have been funded after long peer review. However, when Fleming had his crucial insight on examining the contaminated plate, he would have been faced with a dilemma. Of course, he would have wanted to give up his earlier research and investigate the properties of penicillin, but he would have been aware that changing his research plans in this way might well result in severe penalties from the funding body, penalties which might have been very damaging to his future research career. Thus funding based on the AHRB (2001) model would certainly have discouraged Fleming from taking the steps which led to one of the greatest advances in the history of medicine.

Sometimes Fleming's success is attributed to luck, and certainly he was lucky that one of his plates was contaminated by a mould in that very specific way. However, historians have often commented that luck was not enough, and that Fleming showed considerable ingenuity in recognizing the potential value of the contaminated plate, and immediately starting to investigate it. Hare, who was a colleague of Fleming's at the time, mentions (1970, p.55), with characteristic honesty, that Fleming showed the contaminated plate to all the other researchers in the laboratory, but that no one else thought it was of any importance. Contaminated plates were a relatively common occurrence, and were usually discarded. Commentators have often pointed out that a mediocre scientist would almost certainly have discarded the contaminated plate, continued with the research he or she was working on, and failed to discover penicillin. The irony here is that the strategy which AHRB (2001) impose on researchers by threatening heavy penalties to anyone who fails to follow it, that is the strategy of strict adherence to earlier detailed research plans, is precisely the strategy which would have been followed by the mediocre scientist who saw the contaminated plate, but failed to discover penicillin.

This example gives support to the down-shifting hypothesis of Charlton and Andras (**5.4**) that the most able UK scientists are being pressurized into doing routine normal science rather than attempting anything in the way of revolutionary science. Certainly a funding scheme such as AHRB (2001) would have pressurized Fleming into continuing his routine normal science investigation of colour changes in staphylocooci rather than switching to the revolutionary investigation of penicillin.

That concludes my discussion of the example of Fleming's discovery of penicillin. However, a defender of AHRB (2001) might object that it is not really relevant, because Fleming was a scientist carrying out experimental research in medicine, whereas AHRB (2001) is a funding scheme designed for research in the humanities. I would reply that, in this respect, research in the humanities does not differ significantly from research in the sciences, and will now demonstrate this by my second example which concerns research in philosophy.

10.4 Second Example: Russell's Development of the Logicist Philosophy of Mathematics

One of the most famous British philosophers of the twentieth century was Bertrand Russell. Russell's best research in theoretical philosophy was carried out between 1900 and 1913. During these years, Russell worked on the *logicist* research programme which had been begun by Frege. The idea of this programme was to try to show that mathematics could be reduced to logic. Russell, on examining Frege's earlier attempt to establish logicism, discovered in 1901 that there was a fundamental contradiction in Frege's system. This is now known as *Russell's paradox*. Russell attempted to devise a new logicist system which would overcome this paradox, and this led him to his theory of types which was published in 1908. In this period, Russell also invented his theory of descriptions, which was published in 1905. Working with a colleague (Whitehead), Russell gave a detailed development of his new logicist system in the three monumental volumes of *Principia Mathematica*, which were published between 1910 and 1913. Few would deny that all this constituted exceptionally brilliant philosophical research. We must next examine whether a funding regime like AHRB (2001) would have helped Russell carry out this research, or, whether (as will obviously turn out to be the case!) it would have put obstacles in his path.

To form a judgement on this matter, we must first look at the course of Russell's studies from his arrival at Cambridge in 1890 as an undergraduate student until the beginning of his great period of research in theoretical philosophy from 1900 to 1913. Russell himself gives an account of this in his 1959 book: *My Philosophical Development*. Russell began by studying mathematics for three years from 1890 to 1893. He then devoted a year to studying philosophy. Cambridge at that period was under the influence of German idealism, and Russell tells us (1959, p.38) that his teachers 'with one single exception' who was 'regarded ... as out of date' were 'either Kantian or Hegelian'. After finishing his undergraduate studies, a student like Russell would nowadays proceed to a PhD, but there was no such degree in Cambridge at that time, and the next step then was to write a fellowship dissertation. Russell chose as the topic for his dissertation 'The Foundations of Geometry', and perhaps not surprisingly in view of his undergraduate education chose a Kantian approach. In 1896, he published a revised version of his fellowship dissertation as the book: *An Essay on the Foundations of Geometry*. Writing in 1959 he is somewhat unkind to this early effort and says (p. 39): 'My first philosophical book ... seems to me now somewhat foolish.' A little later he says (1959, p. 40):

'However, there was worse to follow. My theory of geometry was mainly Kantian, but after this I plunged into efforts at Hegelian dialectic. I wrote a paper "On the Relations of Number of Quantity" which is unadulterated Hegel.'

Russell quotes the first two paragraphs of this article and comments (1959, p. 41): ' ... it seems to me now nothing but unmitigated rubbish.'

At the time, however, Russell was an enthusiastic Hegelian, and began an elaborate project for giving a Hegelian account of the foundations of physics. In 1959, he gives the following assessment of this work (p. 43):

'On re-reading what I wrote about the philosophy of physics in the years 1896 to 1898, it seems to me complete nonsense, and I find it hard to imagine how I can ever have thought otherwise. Fortunately, before any of this work had reached a stage where I thought it fit for publication, I changed my whole philosophy and proceeded to forget all that I had done in those two years.'

So Russell completely changed his approach between 1898, when he was still a Hegelian, and 1900, when he had abandoned Hegelianism and adopted the logicist approach to the philosophy of mathematics.

Now let us suppose that Russell had applied early in 1898 for funding to a board similar to the AHRB and operating with the principles of AHRB (2001). Of course this is completely anachronistic for 1898, but is quite realistic for a contemporary researcher. By 1898, Russell had reached about the stage at which a contemporary researcher in philosophy has just completed his or her PhD and may be looking for support for post-doctoral research from a body giving funding for the humanities. If Russell had indeed applied early in 1898, he would have described his research project as being that of developing a Hegelian approach to physics. He would also have been likely to get the award, since Hegelian philosophy was quite dominant in the UK at that moment, and indeed many of Russell's teachers at Cambridge were Hegelian. But now let us suppose that, shortly after receiving his award and continuing with his Hegelian work, Russell suddenly reaches the conclusion that it is, in his own words, 'unmitigated rubbish' and 'complete nonsense'.

His study of Peano and conversations with G.E.Moore have convinced him, almost certainly correctly, that it would be much more fruitful to try to develop a logicist approach to the philosophy of mathematics than a Hegelian approach to the philosophy of physics. This, of course, is exactly what occurred, and, at that time 1898-1900, this change of opinion caused no problem for Russell. He simply started working on his new project with the successful results which we have described earlier.

If, however, Russell had depended for his support on a grant awarded under the conditions of AHRB (2001), things would not have been so easy for him. He would have been faced with a very difficult choice. The first option would have been to continue with his original Hegelian plan. This would have satisfied the conditions of the award, but it would have been difficult to continue with an approach which he now regarded as 'complete nonsense'. Moreover he would, as we can now see in retrospect, have damaged his chances of making the striking discoveries for which he was to become famous. The second option would have been to abandon the Hegelian plan and start work on the new logicist project. However, if he had done this, Russell would have become liable to the penalties so clearly specified in AHRB (2001). He would have been barred altogether from applying for further funding for two years, and as AHRB (2001) says clearly that (p. 20): 'we will keep a record of the unsatisfactory assessment on file, and this will be taken into consideration when you make further applications to the AHRB', it is very likely that Russell would not have obtained any further funding after his award ceased. Supposing this had been in 1901, then Russell would have been ineligible for any funding from Britain's major funding body in the humanities during the period (1901-13) when he carried out his greatest research in theoretical philosophy (the theory of descriptions, the theory of types, and the elaboration of his version of the logicist philosophy of mathematics). The conclusion is inescapable that a funding regime along the lines of AHRB (2001) would have placed major obstacles in the way of Russell carrying out his major research projects in theoretical philosophy, and might indeed have prevented him from so doing altogether.

At this point a defender of AHRB (2001) might say that I am being unfair, because so far I have not mentioned that they do at one point consider the possibility of significant modifications of the research plan. The passage runs as follows (p. 18):

'You may encounter circumstances which require you to modify significantly the research plan and its aims and objectives. In such cases you must obtain the prior approval of the Board before implementing any modifications.'

Thus, if Fleming had been operating with a funding regime such as AHRB (2001), he could have applied to the Board for approval of the modification of his research plan from investigating colour changes in staphylococci to investigating the properties of penicillin. One can hardly suppress a wry smile when imagining the scene. Fleming has just had the basic insight that his contaminated culture-plate might be the key to providing a major new medical therapy. Filled with excitement, he starts investigating whether this is the case or not. But then he remembers the Funding Board's requirements, abandons his research, and sits down to compose a humble note to the Board to request permission to be allowed to carry out his new researches. This, it will be remembered, is a Board, part of whose mission statement was 'to enhance ... the creative output of the nation'. The situation is indeed a ridiculous one, but the smile should be wry rather than genuine since it is perfectly possible, indeed likely, that the board would not give permission for the modification of the research plan. We can see this by examining the case of Russell.

If Russell in say 1899 had applied to the Board for permission to change his research plan from the Hegelian to the logicist one, what would the Board have done? Their most likely reaction would have been to consult the peer reviewers who had approved Russell's original project. Now, as I pointed out earlier, these peer reviewers would have been likely to be Hegelian philosophers, and, as such, they would very probably have judged that Russell's original plan was better than his new one. Russell records (1959, p. 38) that the teacher who influenced him most in philosophy when he was a student was the Hegelian McTaggart. Later on, however, the relations between the two men did not remain very cordial. Russell developed the new analytic philosophy based on Frege's logic, and this replaced Hegelianism as the dominant philosophy at Cambridge. Moreover the two men disagreed during the First World War which McTaggart supported while Russell became a pacifist. In his 1956 book: *Portraits from Memory*, Russell speaking of McTaggart describes (p. 67):

' ... an occasion during the first war, when he asked me no longer to come and see him because he could not bear my opinions. He followed this up by taking a leading part in having me turned out of my lectureship.'

Would such a man have approved the younger Russell's wish to change his research plan from Hegelianism to logicism?

10.5 General Conclusions regarding AHRB (2001)

Generalising from the examples of Fleming and Russell, we can easily see why the strategy of strict adherence to earlier detailed research plans, which

AHRB (2001) imposes on researchers with heavy penalties if they disobey, is almost certain to diminish the quality of the research produced. In research what we want are of course major advances, exciting innovations, and big breakthroughs. However, these will almost certainly be accompanied by a change in the researcher's earlier plans. The effect of AHRB (2001) will thus, like the RAE, be to push all research towards the routine research of normal science, resulting in slow progress and small advances.

This argument would seem to be a rather obvious one, and equally, if not more, obvious is the fact that by imposing extra administrative burdens on the research community, AHRB (2001) would drive up the costs of research. One cannot help wondering why the AHRB introduced a new scheme which so clearly results in a double worsening of the research. Unfortunately this question is difficult to answer. If the AHRB had encouraged an open discussion in the research community of the new scheme before introducing it, then arguments for and against the scheme would have emerged, and we would have learnt the reasons why the AHRB thought that the new scheme would result in an improvement of the research produced. However, the new scheme was introduced and imposed on the research community without anything in the way of an open discussion of its merits. Moreover the authors of the scheme were, and remain, anonymous, and they do not, in describing the new scheme they are imposing, give any reasons for supposing that it would be an improvement on the old scheme. Such reasons must have existed, however, as it is impossible to believe that the authors of AHRB (2001) acted in an entirely arbitrary fashion. If we are to reconstruct these reasons, we have to enter the realm of conjecture, but there is quite a plausible conjecture which I will expound in the next chapter (Chapter 11). My guess, for which I will give arguments, is that that the authors of AHRB (2001) were in the grip of what I will call: **the supermarket fallacy**. Let us turn now to a consideration of this fallacy.

Chapter 11. Improving Administration and Management: (ii) the Supermarket Fallacy

11.1 Statement of the Fallacy

Let me begin by explaining what I mean by 'the supermarket fallacy'. Supermarkets are among some of the most successful companies in the modern world. From small beginnings many have grown to become large multi-national enterprises with outlets all over the world. In the course of this expansion, they have made large profits which have enabled them to pay a large stream of dividends to their shareholders. All this would scarcely have been possible if supermarket managers had not used methods to make their enterprises highly efficient. All this so far has been undeniable. The fallacy now comes in the claim that the managerial methods which have made supermarkets efficient would improve the efficiency of research organisations if they were to adopt them. This is a fallacy, of course, because it by no means follows that managerial methods which improve the efficiency of supermarkets would also improve the efficiency of research organisations if they were applied there. The activities of supermarkets are very different from those of research, and it could well be that these different activities require different managerial methods to produce efficiency. In fact, I will now show that this is indeed the case, and that the very managerial methods which increase efficiency in supermarkets, have exactly the opposite effect if applied to research. Such managerial methods decrease rather increase the efficiency of research production. To demonstrate this, I will begin in the next section with an analysis of a core supermarket activity, namely shelf stacking.

11.2 Analysis of Shelf Stacking

As the customers pass through the aisles of a supermarket removing commodities from the shelves, these shelves have to be re-filled. A group of workers is employed on this task, and their activities are very familiar to the general public. Let us now examine the managerial methods which might be employed to improve the efficiency of these workers. To take a simple numerical example, let us suppose that there are 100 shelf stackers. Of these 100 workers, 80 are conscientious and hard-working and do as much shelf stacking in their working day as could reasonably be expected. However, human nature being what it is, there are also 20 workers who are not so conscientious and hard-working, and try to do as little shelf stacking as they can get away with. We can imagine that they use all sorts of devices to escape work, such as going off to the bathroom to have a smoke etc. As a result these 20 workers do only half as much shelf stacking as the hard-working majority.

In a unit period of time for which the workers receive a unit of wages, let us suppose that the 80 hard-working shelf stackers do each a unit of shelf stacking. Then the 100 workers at a cost of 100 will produce an output of 90. So the efficiency is 90%.

How could the management improve this efficiency? Well, as we have seen, 20 workers are avoiding work. Thus if the amount of work avoidance could be reduced, efficiency might improve. So the management is likely to introduce strategies for reducing the avoidance of work, or StRAWs for short. Let us suppose that two low-level managers are appointed to implement these strategies. If the workers receive one unit of wages per unit of time, it is reasonable to suppose that these managers will receive two units of wages. Managers always have to be paid more than workers to exclude the possibility that they side with the workers against the higher managers, shareholders etc. Now the point to note is that costs have now increased from 100 to 104. So to improve efficiency, there has to be a considerable improvement in output. This can only be achieved in our example by increasing the output of the 20 work-avoiding workers. This was initially 10. Let us see the effects of increasing this output first to 14, then to 16, and then to 18. If the output goes up to 14, the total output becomes 94, but the costs have risen to 104. So the efficiency (= 94/104) becomes 90.4%. This is a negligible increase, and so it would seem hardly worth the trouble of appointing the two managers. Similar calculations show that for an increase to 16, the efficiency rises to 92.3%, and for an increase to 18, the efficiency rises to 94.2%. So if the two new managers can increase the output of the 20 work-avoiding workers to a sufficiently high level, they have definitely justified their employment in terms of increased efficiency.

It is worth noting, however, that there is a limit to improvements in efficiency which can be achieved by appointing managers. The maximum improvement in the output of the 20 work avoiding workers is from 10 to 20, which would bring total output up to 100. Suppose that, to achieve this result, it was necessary to appoint 5 managers. Costs would now have risen from 100 to 110 and so efficiency would now only be 100/110 or 90.9%. Thus there would be only a negligible increase in efficiency. The situation in which 6 managers are appointed would be even worse, since now the efficiency would only be 100/112 or 89.3%. So the efficiency would be less with 6 managers than it would have been with no managers at all.

This simple example thus clearly illustrates an important concept which I will refer to as **managerial or administrative degeneration**. Such degeneration occurs when the costs of managers and administration outweighs any compensating increase in output, so that the system becomes less efficient than it would be with fewer managers and less administration.

11.3 Strategies for Reducing the Avoidance of Work (StRAWs)

In our simple shelf stacking example, we remarked that the newly appointed managers would have to implement strategies for reducing the avoidance of work (or StRAWs). Now what might these strategies be? There are at least two in common use, namely (i) surveillance, and (ii) making the worker accountable. I will consider them in turn.

Surveillance is an obvious strategy. No doubt our two newly appointed managers would prowl the aisles of the supermarket to check that the shelf stackers are really stacking shelves, and not, e.g. pausing to have a chat with a fellow shelf stacker on some topic of mutual interest such as the performance of the local football team. Charlie Chaplin parodies this kind of managerial activity in an amusing fashion in his film *Modern Times* (1936). In this film Charlie is a worker on a production line in a giant factory. At one point he decides to take a break, and goes to the bathroom. Here he lights up a cigarette, and settles down to relax and enjoy it, when suddenly the whole wall behind him lights up as a giant screen. An image of the manager of the whole factory appears, causing Charlie to jump out of his skin. The manager says: 'Hey! Quit stalling. Get back to your work. Go on!' Charlie immediately rushes out of the bathroom. There is one little subtlety about the way this episode is portrayed which might be missed. Charlie in fact clocks out before entering the bathroom, and clocks in again after leaving. So he is not in fact taking a break in time for which he is being paid. Nonetheless he is ordered back to his work in a peremptory fashion.

Let us now turn to the second of our common strategies – that of making the worker accountable. This can be easily implemented for shelf stackers. A particular shelf stacker is made responsible for ensuring that some specified shelves do not become empty. If they do become empty, then the shelf stacker is held accountable and a penalty is imposed. For example, the shelf stacker may lose a bonus. This is a more efficient method from the management point of view since continuous surveillance is no longer necessary. Instead there can be a system of occasional random checks. However, the worker, not knowing when these checks will occur, has to keep working continuously for fear of losing his or her bonus.

These common strategies then work well in the supermarket context, but do they work well in the research context? This is the question to which we must now turn.

11.4 Can Supermarket-like Managerial Strategies be applied to Research Workers?

The first difficulty about transferring supermarket-like managerial strategies to the research context is that it is very hard to implement them in this new context. To see this, let us consider in turn how the two common strategies of (i) surveillance, and (ii) making the worker accountable might be applied to research workers.

As we saw, it was very easy to apply surveillance to a shelf stacker. All that was needed was for a manager to prowl the aisles of the supermarket to see if the shelf stacker was indeed working. But could we apply the same technique to, for example, a research mathematician who is supposed to be carrying out research in his subject at home? Let us suppose that we could fit up surveillance cameras in the researcher's home and neighbourhood, so that the doings of the researcher, whom I will suppose to be a man, can be observed by a manager in the university. What does this manager observe on a particular day? First of all he sees the mathematician lazying about in bed until mid-day. He then gets up, and treats himself to a leisurely brunch. After this, he goes for a long walk in a nearby park, and has a cup of tea in the park's café. It is not till nearly five o'clock that he returns to his house, sits down at his desk and spends an hour writing down obscure formulas. The conclusion seems inescapable. The research mathematician instead of working a full day has worked only for one hour.

However, when the manager confronts the research mathematician with his finding, the mathematician cannot help smiling. 'You have got it all wrong' he replies. 'The day you mention was the most productive of my entire life. As a result of intense thought I formulated the basic equations of the $\omega\sigma$-calculus, which I am convinced will create a new branch of mathematics of great practical importance. When lying in bed in the morning I was thinking about mathematical problems. In fact Descartes, one of the greatest mathematicians of all time, used to lie in bed till midday every day thinking about mathematical problems. My mind was similarly totally occupied with mathematics when I was walking in the park. The day you mention was one of the most intense work that I can remember, but fortunately the work was very fruitful.' Now what is the manager to make of this? It could be true, but then it could be all a lie. Those formulas which the mathematician wrote down could be just a smokescreen to conceal the fact that he had really spent the day in idleness, or they could indeed be the key equations of an important new branch of mathematics. How is the manager to tell?

Here there seems to be only one answer, namely to resort to peer review. The mysterious formulas are sent to some suitable referees to give their opinion.

If the answer comes back, that they represent brilliant work, then perhaps the mathematician will be believed. But suppose the referees think that the allegedly important ωσ-calculus is really something of no importance. Has our mathematician finally been caught out? Not necessarily. As we saw earlier, Frege's introduction of the propositional and predicate calculi was judged by his peers to be of no significance, whereas, nowadays, it is seen to be the foundation of an important branch of mathematics (mathematical logic) which was vital for the development of computer science (**2.2** and **5.1**). Our mathematician, who we are supposing to be quite knowledgeable about the history of mathematics, might make this comparison, and say that the referees chosen by the manager have simply failed to appreciate the significance of his ωσ-calculus, just because it is such a big innovation.

All this shows that the technique of surveillance, which was so easy to use in the supermarket, is very difficult to apply to research workers. The same holds for that other well-known strategy of making the worker accountable.

In the supermarket case, the aim of shelf stackers is clear. They have to ensure that the shelves are always filled with commodities which the customers may want to buy. If a shelf is empty, then it can be seen at a glance that this aim has not been achieved. Hence it is easy to make shelf stackers accountable for keeping shelves full. But now compare this situation with that of research workers. The aim of research workers is to produce good research. However, we certainly cannot see at a glance whether this aim has been achieved or not. In fact as long as thirty years may have to elapse before we can judge with any certainty whether a particular research worker has carried out good research, or merely produced something ephemeral of no lasting significance. Is it possible, or even desirable, to hold research workers accountable for producing good research? Let us compare the cases of Gottlob Frege (**2.2**) and Frank Abbot (**8.7**). Both worked for years with no recognition, but, whereas, Frege was eventually judged to have done brilliant and important research, Abbot's research was in the long run judged to be a failure. Suppose Frege and Abbot are still alive 30 or 40 years after the beginning of their research careers, and this judgement has now become clear. Should the unfortunate Frank Abbot be held accountable for not having produced good research and be penalised in some way for his failure? Surely this would be quite unreasonable, even if it were possible.

If managers are still keen to apply the strategy of making the worker accountable to research workers, there seems to be only one way in which this can be done, namely to substitute for the research workers' real aim, namely to produce good research, a different and more specific aim for which the research worker really can be held accountable. For example, a research worker could be told that he has to publish so many papers in such and such a period of time in a specific set of journals. The problem with substituting an aim which is different from the real aim of the enterprise is that this may hinder the accomplishment of the real aim. In this case, the research worker may have to give up an unusual line of research which he or she thinks, correctly, will lead to a big advance, because he or she knows the principle that the papers most likely to be accepted by the journal in question are those which add an epicycle to a well-established research programme. Hence the need to accomplish the different substitute aim hinders the accomplishment of the real aim.

Once again, the strategy of making the worker accountable, which could be implemented so easily in the supermarket, is very hard to apply to research workers. These difficulties are not, however, a great cause of concern, because, as I will now show, strategies for reducing the avoidance of work which can indeed raise efficiency to some extent in the supermarket context, always have the opposite effect in the research context and inevitably reduce the efficiency of research activity. So we should not be too worried about the difficulties of implementing strategies which always have a negative effect. The different effects of strategies for reducing the avoidance of work (or StRAWs) in the two cases is due to further differences between the work of shelf stacking and the work of research. I will now go on to discuss these further differences.

11.5 Why StRAWs reduce Efficiency when applied to Research

There are two key respects in which research work differs from the work of shelf stacking. First of all research work is extremely fascinating for those who are good at it, and so successful researchers will always work hard at their research simply because they enjoy it. Admittedly not everyone enjoys research and study, but researchers are nowadays almost exclusively recruited from those who have done very well at school and university. Such success is only likely to come to those who enjoy study, or working in laboratories. So researchers have already been selected as a group who like research. Moreover to succeed well at school and university, habits of hard work must have been developed and these are unlikely to disappear in later life. In addition to all these factors, researchers, in the UK at least, earn only a fraction of what they could get in any other occupation which required the qualifications they have obtained. Why then would they remain researchers if they didn't like research, and a much higher salary could be obtained elsewhere? This is in sharp contrast to shelf stackers whose work is boring and repetitive. There must be a strong temptation for a shelf stacker to try to avoid work in some way, but why should researchers try to avoid the work which they find interesting and enjoyable? It surely follows that avoidance of work is not likely to be a major problem for researchers and consequently that strategies for reducing the avoidance of work, while they have some justification for shelf stackers, are inappropriate for research workers.

This is one key respect in which research work differs from shelf stacking. However, the second difference between the two is even more important. Shelf stacking, though boring and repetitive, can be carried out by any able-bodied person. However, not everyone can carry out successful research. In fact there is a relative minority of people who have the knack of doing research well. Let us examine the consequences of this difference for strategies for reducing work avoidance. In the case of shelf stacking, if someone who had been avoiding his or her work is forced by the StRAW to do more work, his or her work will be just as good as that of anyone else. But now suppose that a particular research worker is not doing much research and we force him or her to do more, will the result be some research just as good as that of those who are working hard at their research? The answer is obviously: 'no'. Why should a particular research worker – I will assume he is a man – not be working hard? There are a variety of possibilities. The most likely reason is that he simply does not have any ideas for further research. He might have been very successful working earlier on a particular research programme, but that programme has run out of steam and he can't think of a new one to work on. In this case, if he was forced to produce some research, he would no doubt be able to write a paper or two, but these papers are unlikely to be very good. Other reasons for a research worker not doing much research might be that he is suffering from a depression, or is tired out by the demands of a young family, or has a psychological research block. These could all be temporary phenomena. The depression might lift, his children might go to kindergarten, and the psychological block might be overcome, so that he would find himself once more able to do good research. However, forcing him to carry out research in the difficult period is very unlikely indeed to produce any good research output. The key point here is that trying to force people to do research is a complete waste of time, and will never result in an improved research output. Those whose research is going well do not need to be forced to do research. They will be pursuing it vigorously without any compulsion being necessary. Almost all the valuable research will come from these researchers. Those who are having difficulties with their research for one or other of the reasons just described, will not be able to produce any research of great value, even if they are forced to work. The contrast here with shelf stacking should be obvious.

However the situation when StRAWs are applied to research workers is not just a waste of time, but positively damaging to research. This is because, as we have seen, the application of a StRAW to research is not simple and straightforward as it is in the case of shelf stacking. Shelf stackers can be easily monitored without interfering with their work, but this is not the case with research workers. To monitor research workers, it is necessary to impose administrative burdens on them. They have to make complicated declarations of what they have been doing and of what they intend to do. The quality of their output has to be assessed by peer review which imposes a heavy burden on the research community as a whole. Such administrative burdens are costly and necessarily result in a reduction of output from the good, successful researchers. This loss of output will not, as just pointed out, be compensated by having some extra poor quality research produced by those who, for whatever reason, are not working very hard at their research. In our earlier analysis of shelf stacking, it was shown that the application of a StRAW might indeed produce an increase in efficiency, but that this would be eroded and turn into a decrease in efficiency if too many managers were appointed. This was called managerial or administrative degeneration. What has now been shown is that any application of a StRAW to research workers immediately produces managerial or administrative degeneration.

Let me conclude with an analogy which should help to make the situation clear. Let us imagine, anachronistically, that at the time of the Italian Renaissance, a group of about twenty artists are receiving a salary from the Florentine government to enable them to pursue their artistic work undisturbed. This group, we can further suppose, includes Michelangelo, Botticelli and other well-known artists. It also, however, includes a couple of rather incompetent artists who spend their salary drinking in the tavern and produce little in the way of art. This sorry state comes to the attention of an efficiency minded Florentine bureaucrat, who decides that a stop must be put to this waste of government funds. He therefore introduces a series of elaborate checks which means that all the artists have to spend about 20% of their time filling in forms etc. As a result of these checks, the two incompetent artists spend less time drinking and produce a few more paintings, which are wretched daubs of no value. However, Michelangelo, Botticelli, and the other brilliant artists of the period have to spend 20% less of their time on their artistic work and so produce 20% less masterpieces of art for their contemporaries and posterity to enjoy. Surely everyone would agree that the scheme of the Florentine bureaucrat had a negative effect. The application of strategies for reducing avoidance of work (StRAWs) to research has a negative effect of exactly the same kind.

11.6 Re-examination of the Case of AHRB (2001)

Let us now return to a consideration of the new research leave scheme introduced by the AHRB in 2001. The basic idea of this scheme is that the candidate has to formulate in detail a research plan for the period of leave. After the leave is over he or she has to submit a report with a copy of the original plan. A comparison is made between what was planned and what was actually done, and, if there is a significant difference, the candidate is penalised. It will be at once obvious that this is a strategy for reducing avoidance of work or StRAW. In fact it is a StRAW of the kind which was called 'making the worker accountable'. In the supermarket context, this takes the form of instructing a shelf stacker to make sure that a particular set of shelves is never empty and then penalising him or her if at any time they are observed by a manger to be empty. A StRAW of this kind may indeed be effective to some extent in the supermarket context, but, as we saw earlier, it is disastrous in the research context where it has the characteristic double worsening effect of driving up research costs through the imposition of administrative burdens on the research community, and driving down the quality of the research produced by enforcing the foolish principle of strict adherence to earlier detailed research plans. My hypothesis is that the mistake of the authors of AHRB (2001) was to try to implement a managerial principle which is indeed successful to some extent in many areas of industrial production and distribution, without realising that this managerial principle has negative effects in the research area. In other words, they were in the grip of the supermarket fallacy. I have called the fallacy 'the supermarket fallacy' because the case of supermarkets is familiar and easy to analyse. However I mean the phase 'supermarket fallacy' to have a more general sense, and to refer to the mistake of supposing that management methods which increase efficiency in the case of an industrial company will have the same effect in a research organisation.

It might, however, be objected that I am being unfair to the authors of AHRB (2001). 'Surely' it could be said, 'these must have been important government officials, or advisers from industry. They would have been educated men and women trusted by the government with raising the efficiency of UK research. Surely such people would have realised the obvious difference between the work of Einstein, Fleming, and Russell, and that of shelf stackers in a supermarket. Surely they would also have realised that different managerial methods would be appropriate in the two cases. How could they have been victims of the supermarket fallacy?' Now I fully concede that once we clearly analyse the differences between shelf stacking and research work, as has been done above, the supermarket fallacy does indeed come to seem a glaring fallacy. However, intelligent people can often fall into fallacious thinking if the fallacies are implicit in some general framework, or view of the world, which they accept. Now in 2001, the dominant ideology in government circles in the UK was that private corporations such as banks or supermarkets are the models of organisational efficiency, and that this efficiency should be transferred to the less efficient public sector. As research belonged largely to the public sector, we can see that this attitude contains implicitly the supermarket fallacy.

The existence of this dominant ideology is demonstrated by the remarkable fact, already noted, that the AHRB actually constituted itself as a company in April 2001 'to allow the AHRB ... to have a more direct relationship with the community it serves.' (AHRB, 2001, p. 5). Moreover the AHRB imitated the annual reports of companies of the time by having a mission statement and a set of strategic priorities. Another indication of the dominant ideology that corporate efficiency should be transferred to the public sector is seen in the appointment of successful managers from industry to head universities and research institutes in the UK. The implicit assumption here is that a manager who has introduced methods which have increased the efficiency of an industrial company will be able to increase the efficiency of a university or research institute in as similar fashion. What is this but the supermarket fallacy?

In reality industrial managers, even if, or perhaps especially if, they have been very successful in running an industrial company, are, on our analysis, likely to have a very negative effect on a university or research institute, just because they are the sort of person most likely to be in the grip of the supermarket fallacy. Our analysis would rather suggest that no one should be appointed to a senior managerial position in a university or research institute who has not spent many years actually engaged in research. Only such a person would know about the many features of research as an activity which are indeed strange and in many ways the opposite of what an outsider might expect. We can illustrate this point with an example.[10]

In 2003 Paul Lauterbur won a Nobel prize jointly with Peter Mansfield for their work in developing Magnetic Resonance Imaging (or MRI). As almost everyone knows nowadays, MRI scans are of enormous benefit in medicine. In his Nobel lecture, Lauterbur revealed that the paper in which he made his key advance was rejected by the leading scientific journal *Nature*. He said (p. 248): '... a manuscript I wrote for the journal *Nature* ... was summarily rejected. I felt this was a mistake, not because I foresaw all of the medical applications that would follow, but because of the physical uniqueness of the concept.' Nicholas Wade writing in an article in *The New York Times* on 7 October 2003 reports Lauterbur as saying: 'You could write the entire history of science in the last 50 years in terms of papers rejected by Science or Nature.' Not many researchers would be quite as outspoken as Lauterbur. Yet anyone who had carried out research for fifteen or twenty years, and especially skilful researchers, would know enough not put too much trust in the peer reviewers of leading journals. Consider by contrast an industrialist who had run a confectionery company very successfully for fifteen or twenty years, but who had never carried out any research. If appointed as a manager of a leading research institute, such a person, who I will assume is a man, might well make terrible blunders. He might learn that peer review is the gold standard for research, and that good research papers are those published in leading journals. As a result, he could well assume that a scientist who had had a paper rejected by *Nature* or *Science* was no good. Worse still, in a misguided attempt to raise the standards of his institute, he could get rid of any young researchers who failed to get their papers accepted in leading journals. In this way, he could inadvertently deprive his institute of future Nobel prize winners, and damage severely the quality of its research output. These mistakes would arise not from any lack of intelligence, but from a lack of familiarity with the subtleties of research as an activity, combined with over-confidence in his own judgement arising out of his successes in running the confectionery company. Later on we will give an example of a very successful research manager who was himself a Nobel prize winner and ran a laboratory in which others went on to win the Nobel prize.

I will now try to give another way of explaining how the supermarket fallacy, existing in an implicit or concealed form, can exercise its baleful influence on research. This uses Kuhn's concept of paradigm, which, as we saw earlier, is very helpful in explaining how experts in a field have been led to make erroneous judgements about new work, later recognised as constituting an important advance. My suggestion is to apply Kuhn's concept to management. Here, however, in contrast to normal science, there would be a number of competing paradigms, each one giving an analysis of what are the principal obstacles to increasing efficiency, as well as strategies for overcoming these obstacles. Now a very entrenched paradigm in management is one which regards the primary task of managers as that of reducing work avoidance. This paradigm was well established in 1936 when it was satirized by Charlie Chaplin. However, it probably goes back to the beginning of the industrial revolution. The organisation of work in factories brought about a new type of boring and repetitive labour. It would be natural for anyone who had to perform such labour to try to avoid work, and hence there emerged the paradigm which we are discussing. Since this paradigm applied well to the new type of labour which came increasingly to be the most common type of labour in society, it was natural that it should become entrenched and dominate the thinking of managers. Hence arose the natural mistake of applying this paradigm to an area for which it was quite unsuited.

However, for research work, a new paradigm is needed. This could be characterised as holding that the primary task for research managers is to remove obstacles to work. The situation here is in many ways the opposite of factory production. Instead of having a bored work force, many of whom are only too anxious to avoid work, we have an enthusiastic work force, most of whom really enjoy what they are doing, and would like to spend as much time as possible on it. Some of these research workers, but we don't in advance know which ones, will produce great progress in their field. The task of the research manager is to remove any obstacles which may stand in the way of these enthusiastic workers doing the work they enjoy. In so doing, the research manager will ensure that the big contributors, who are not yet known, will not be held up in making their contributions.

The big difficulty, as I see it, is to change thinking from the familiar managerial paradigm of reducing work avoidance to the new paradigm of removing obstacles to work. Once the new paradigm is accepted, it will be an easy matter to implement it in practice and produce great improvements in the research enterprise as a whole. I will now briefly sketch why this is so.

11.7 The Paradigm of Removing Obstacles to Work

The managerial paradigm of removing obstacles to research work is hardly something new. It informed the practice of the best research managers of the past, and it is rather a feature of the last three decades that it has been swept away under the influence of the supermarket fallacy. A 2005 article by Peter Matthews with the significant title: 'Where are we going? Can originality survive our current managerial procedures?' gives an interesting contrast between the old and new styles of research management. He illustrates the new style by quoting the following letter to one of his colleagues at Oxford (2005, p. 4):

'*Dear X,*
You will recall that during the Summer, the Division began a review of its research profile for RAE purposes and that a Working Group was appointed to assist with this work. ... [it] has attempted to assemble relevant data about research activity and in your case not only has your grant income been very low in recent years but also the cumulative impact factor of your best publications during this period also seems to be very low. I should like to invite you to meet me to discuss this. ... The purpose of the meeting is i) to review your publications since the last RAE and ii) to discuss producing a plan for improving your research performance. We shall need to think in the context of this plan about setting some immediate goals for the coming year.'

Matthews comments (p. 4):

'This probably standard letter was signed by the divisional chairman (whose scientific experience bore no relation to that of "X", thereby precluding him from discussing or personally assessing X's actual work with any proper understanding.'

This letter provides very strong evidence for the hypothesis of Charlton and Andras that top UK scientists are being forced to 'down-shift'. Charlton writes (2008, p. 4):

' ... my hunch is that these top-notch Oxford scientists are not being encouraged to do the best work of which they are capable. They are not being encouraged to tackle the biggest scientific problems which they have a chance of solving.

Indeed, it is worse than mere lack of encouragement to do top quality scientific work, it is a matter of positive pressure to down-shift to second-class work. Maybe they are not even being allowed to take the risks entailed by aiming high.'

Let us consider X, one of the recipients at Oxford of the above 'standard letter'. I will suppose that X is a woman. What might she in fact be doing? She could well have decided to work on a minority research programme. This would explain why the cumulative impact factor of her best publications is low. As already pointed out (**6.2**), those working on minority research programmes are less likely to get their work cited by as many researchers as those working in majority research programmes, and so are likely to do worse on citation indices. Moreover it would also explain why she has not been able to get so much grant income, since grants are decided by peer review and so are more likely to be won by those working on majority research programmes (**3.2**).

How could X achieve the goals being imposed by her divisional manager? The obvious strategy would be to switch to working on a majority research programme, and to seek to add some epicycles to a well-established discussion. This would increase her chances of getting papers accepted by leading journals (**4.3**) which would in turn increase her chances of being cited and so doing well on citation indices. These 'improvements' would in turn increase X's chance of getting research grants. If X was a well-established researcher, she might resist managerial pressure, but if X were a young researcher on a temporary contract, she might have to yield just in order to keep her job, and have some chance of a research career. Yet X's wish to pursue the minority research programme could well be justified. It might happen that this minority approach, considered unpromising by most researchers, turned out to be the very one which led to major advances. As we pointed out earlier (**3.2**), zur Hausen who won a Nobel prize in 2008 pursued for many years a minority research programme which was thought by most of his contemporary researchers to have little chance of success, but which nonetheless delivered the goods. If zur Hausen had been a young researcher in contemporary Oxford, he might well have been forced by his departmental manager to 'down-shift' and would never have won the Nobel prize. All this strongly supports the 'down-shifting' hypothesis of Charlton and Andras. It is certainly not difficult to predict that the unfortunate members of the division in question are unlikely to win any Nobel prizes or indeed produce any outstanding research work. The best that could be hoped for is a large number of competent but boring routine papers.

Matthews contrasts this contemporary research manager at Oxford with someone he regards as one of the most successful research managers in history – Max Perutz. Perutz himself won a Nobel prize for his work in determining the structure of haemoglobin, but he also as Matthews points out (p. 5): 'ran one of Britain's most successful laboratories ever.' Matthews describes Perutz's managerial career as follows (p. 5):

' ... the Medical Research Council ... employ[ed] him as the head of of a small new research unit for the study of the Molecular Structure of Biological Systems. This went from strength to strength with its members winning a string of Nobel prizes for a variety of work. Crick came to Perutz as a research student, stayed on, and was later joined there by Watson; the success achieved by their ill-disciplined work habits is well known. Perutz himself with his colleagues, after making many technical and analytical improvements and aided by the advent of powerful computers, eventually successfully determined the three dimensional structure of haemoglobin; they then moved on to study the abnormal haemoglobins found in human disease. Perutz also had to manage the rest of his expanding, vigorous MRC unit. He did this on the basis that he with his board "never directed the laboratory's research but tried to attract talented young people and give them a free hand. My job was to take an [personal] interest in the research, and to make sure that they had the means to carry it out."'

Here in two sentences Perutz sums up the basic principles of good research management. The quotation shows that these principles were known, but that this knowledge was lost when they were replaced by much worse principles. Such a change for the worse could only occur under the influence of a powerful and highly misleading management ideology. This is what I have attempted to characterise as the supermarket fallacy.

Perutz sees his job as being that of making sure that the young talented researchers had the means to carry out their research. This obviously accords completely with what I have called the management paradigm of removing obstacles to work. I will now show that, if this paradigm were to be accepted it could be implemented with great ease.

The main obstacle to research in the U.K. at the moment is the administrative burden imposed on researchers. So, applying the paradigm, the primary task of management should be to remove this burden. This is not in principle difficult since most of the administration imposed on researchers is not only not necessary but even harmful.

Let us consider our standard example of AHRB (2001). This scheme must have been difficult to devise and implement. The guide to the scheme is 28 pages long, and there are a further 3 pages of notes to explain to the applicant how to fill in the application form. The beauty of our new paradigm is that instead of introducing more complexity, it enables us to simplify and this is usually much easier to do. As has been shown, all the innovations introduced by AHRB (2001) were negative, and so a first obvious step would be to do away with them. However, simplifications could be carried much further than this. As we saw, a prerequisite for the AHRB (2001) scheme was that the researcher had already been granted a term of research leave by his or her institution. What really is the point of having the second term of research leave granted by a complicated and fallible procedure which differs from the procedure used for the first term? The funds given by the government to fund the AHRB (2001) research leave scheme could be given directly to the universities, enabling them to allow their staff more research leave. This would do away at a stroke with an unnecessary layer of management and a whole host of complicated administrative procedures.

Whereas schemes like AHRB (2001) brought about a double worsening of the situation, simplifications introduced using the paradigm of removing obstacles to work would, by contrast, produce double improvements, since they would not only improve the quality of research but reduce its cost.

Notes

1. A detailed comparison of the *Begriffsschrift* with the treatment of the corresponding material in Mendelson (1964) and Bell and Machover (1977) is to be found in Gillies, 1992, pp. 275-6.

2. This account of Semmelweis's research is a shortened version of the one given in my paper: Gillies (2005). That paper also contains more detailed references to the considerable literature on Semmelweis. Semmelweis's own account of his researches in Semmelweis (1861) is also worth consulting.

3. A more detailed account of Copernicus' work on astronomy is to be found in Kuhn (1957).

4. For more details, see Gillies (1992).

5. For more details, see Gillies (2005).

6. For more details about the Manchester Digital machine and its claim to be the first computer in the modern sense, see Gillies and Zheng, 2001, pp. 445-9.

7. These details about Fleming and the Royal Society are taken from Macfarlane, 1984, pp. 140-1 and p. 202. (See also note 9 below.)

8. My sketch of Einstein's life up to 1905 is based on the admirable account to be found in Miller, 2001, Ch. 3, pp. 41-83 & Ch. 6, pp. 179-213. I will give several quotations from this source.

9. For Fleming's discovery of penicillin, Hare (1970) is essential reading since Hare was working in the same laboratory as Fleming at the time when the discovery was made. Macfarlane (1984) is an excellent historical account. I have used the example of Fleming's discovery of pencillin to discuss problems of induction and falsification in my (1993), pp. 39-48, and in my (2006b) to present a development of Kuhn's theory of discovery in science. Here, I use the same example to show the absurdity of the research strategy imposed by AHRB (2001).

10. I would like to thank Mark Gillies for drawing this example to my attention.

References

AHRB (2001) Arts and Humanities Research Board. Guide to the Research Leave Scheme. September 2001.

Anderson, A.R. (ed.) (1964) *Minds and Machines*, Prentice-Hall.

Annan, N. (1999) *The Dons*, HarperCollins.

Bacon, F. (1620) *Novum Organum*, English Translation in R.L.Ellis and J. Spedding (eds.), *The Philosophical Works of Francis Bacon*, Routledge, 1905, pp. 212-387.

Bell, J.L. and Machover, M. (1977) *A Course in Mathematical Logic*, North-Holland.

Braben, D.W. (2004) *Pioneering Research. A Risk Worth Taking*, John Wiley.

Bynum, T.W. (ed.) (1972) *Gottlob Frege. Conceptual Notation and Related Articles,* Oxford University Press.

Carnap, R. (1963) Intellectual Autobiography. In P.A.Schilpp (ed.), *The Philosophy of Rudolf Carnap*, Library of Living Philosophers, Open Court, pp. 3-84.

Cellucci, C. & Gillies, D. (eds.) (2005) *Mathematical Reasoning and Heuristics*, King's College Publications.

Charlton, B.G. (2008) What has the RAE ever done for Oxford University? Improvement in normal science – but decline in revolutionary science, *The Oxford Magazine*, **271**, pp. 3-5.

Charlton, B.G., and Andras, P. (2008) 'Down-shifting' among top UK scientists? - The decline of 'revolutionary science' and the rise of 'normal science' in the UK compared with the USA, *Medical Hypotheses*, **70**, pp. 465-472.

Corbyn, Z. (2007) Tough new hurdle for top researchers, THES, 23 November, pp. 1 & 8.

Corbyn, Z. (2008a) DIUS abandons plans for different REF Systems to judge sciences and arts, THE, 24 April, p. 4.

Corbyn, Z. (2008b) Unpaid peer review is worth £1.9 bn, THE, 29 May, p. 17.

Davis, M. (1988a) Mathematical Logic and the Origin of Modern Computing. In Rolf Herken (ed.), *The Universal Turing Machine. A Half-Century Survey*, Oxford University Press, pp. 149-74.

Davis, M. (1988b) Influences of Mathematical Logic on Computer Science. In Rolf Herken (ed.), *The Universal Turing Machine. A Half-Century Survey*, Oxford University Press, pp. 315-26.

Edmonds, D. and Eidinow, J. (2001) *Wittgenstein's Poker. The Story of a Ten-Minute Argument between two Great Philosophers,* faber and faber.

Einstein, A. (1905) Zur Elektrodynamik bewegter Körper, *Annalen der Physik*, **17**, pp. 891-921. (English Translation as 'On the Electrodynamics of Moving Bodies'. In *The Principle of Relativity*, Dover Publications, Inc., 1952, pp. 35-71.)

Fleming, A. (1929) On the Antibacterial Action of Cultures of a Penicillium, with Special Reference to their Use in the Isolation of *B. Influenzae*, *British Journal of Experimental Pathology*, **10**, pp. 226-236.

Frege, G. (1879) *Begriffsschrift, eine der Arithmetischen nachgebildete Formelsprache des reinen Denkens*. English translation in Bynum (1972), pp. 101-203.

Frey, B.S. (2003) Publishing as prostitution? - Choosing between one's own ideas and academic success, *Public Choice*, **116**, pp. 205-223.

Frey, B.S. and Osterloh, M. (2008) Evaluations: Hidden Costs, Questionable Benefits, and Superior Alternatives, *Working Paper*, Institute of Empirical Research in Economics, University of Zurich.

Gillies, D. (ed.) (1992) *Revolutions in Mathematics*, Oxford University Press.

Gillies, D. (1992) The Fregean Revolution in Logic. In D. Gillies (ed.), 1992, pp. 265-305.

Gillies, D. (1993) *Philosophy of Science in the Twentieth Century. Four Central Themes*, Blackwell.

Gillies, D. (2002) Logicism and the Development of Computer Science. In Antonis C.Kakas and Fariba Sadri (eds.) *Computational Logic:Logic*

Programming and Beyond, Part II, Springer, pp. 588-604.

Gillies, D. (2005) Hempelian and Kuhnian approaches in the Philosophy of Medicine: the Semmelweis case, *Studies in History and Philosophy of Biological and Biomedical Sciences*, **36**, pp. 159-181.

Gillies, D. (2006a) Why research assessment exercises are a bad thing, *Post-Autistic Economics Review*, **37**, 28 April, article 1, pp. 2-9. http://www.paecon.net/PAEReview/issue37/Gillies37.htm.

Gillies, D. (2006b) Kuhn on Discovery and the Case of Penicillin. In Wenceslao J. Gonzalez and Jesus Alcolea (eds.) *Contemporary Perspectives in Philosophy and Methodology of Science*, Net biblo, S.L., pp. 47-63.

Gillies, D. (2007) Lessons from the History and Philosophy of Science regarding the Research Assessment Exercise. In Anthony O'Hear (ed.) *Philosophy of Science*, Cambridge University Press, pp. 37-73.

Gillies, D. and Zheng, Y. (2001) Dynamic Interactions with the Philosophy of Mathematics, *Theoria*, **16**, pp. 437-59.

Grosholz, E. & Breger, H. (eds.) (2000) *The Growth of Mathematical Knowledge*, Kluwer.

Hare, R. (1970) *The Birth of Penicillin and the Disarming of Microbes*, Allen & Unwin.

Hempel, C.G. (1966) *Philosophy of Natural Science*, Prentice-Hall.

Ietto-Gillies, G. (2008) A XXI-century alternative to XX-century peer review, *real-world economics review*, **45**, pp. 10-22. http://www.paecon.net/PAEReview/issue45/IettoGillies45.pdf

Jones, P. (ed.) (2000) *George Rylands 1902-99. A Memoir.* Printed for King's College, Cambridge.

Kuhn, T.S. (1957) *The Copernican Revolution*, Vintage, 1959.

Kuhn. T.S. (1962) *The Structure of Scientific Revolutions*, University of Chicago Press, 1969.

Kuklick, B. (1977) *The Rise of American Philosophy. Cambridge, Massachusetts, 1860-1930,* Yale University Press, Second Printing, 1979.

135

Lauterbur, P.C. (2003) All Science is Interdisciplinary – From Magnetic Moments to Molecules to Men, *Nobel Lecture,* December 8.

Lucas, J.R. (1961) Minds, Machines and Gödel, *Philosophy*, **36**. Reprinted in Anderson, 1964, pp. 43-59.

Macfarlane, G. (1984) *Alexander Fleming. The Man and the Myth*, Chatto & Windus

Malcolm, N. (1958) *Ludwig Wittgenstein. A Memoir*, 2nd Edition, Oxford University Press, 1989.

Matthews, P. (2005) Where are we going? Can originality survive our current managerial procedures? *The Oxford Magazine*, **236**, pp. 4-6.

Maxwell, N. (2007) *From Knowledge to Wisdom. A Revolution for Science and the Humanities,* Second Edition, Blackwell.

Mendelson, E. (1964) *Introduction to Mathematical Logic*, Van Nostrand.

Miller, A.I. (2001) *Einstein, Picasso*, Basic Books.

Monk, R. (1990) *Ludwig Wittgenstein. The Duty of Genius*, Jonathan Cape.

Numerico, T. and Bowen, J. (2007) Open Science, Wikipedia, the commons, and hierarchical peer reviewed evaluation methods, Abstract of a talk given at the *5th Annual European Computing and Philosophy Conference*, University of Twente, Netherlands, June 21-23, 2007.

Pitcher, G. (1964) *The Philosophy of Wittgenstein*, Prentice-Hall.

Russell, B. (1956) *Portraits from Memory and Other Essays*, George Allen and Unwin.

Russell, B. (1959) *My Philosophical Development*, George Allen and Unwin.

Semmelweis, I. (1861) *The Etiology, Concept, and Prophylaxis of Childbed Fever*. English Translation by K. Codell Carter, The University of Wisconsin Press, 1983.

THE Abbreviation for *Times Higher Education*

THES Abbreviation for *Times Higher Education Supplement*

Turing, A.M. (1950) Computing Machinery and Intelligence, *Mind*, **59**. Reprinted in Anderson, 1964, pp. 4-30.

Wade, N. (2003) American and Briton Win Nobel for Using Chemists' Test for M.R.I.'s, *The New York Times*, October 7.

Wittgenstein, L. (1953) *Philosophical Investigations,* English Translation by G.E.M.Anscombe, Blackwell, 1963.

www.ingramcontent.com/pod-product-compliance
Lightning Source LLC
Chambersburg PA
CBHW070923270326
41927CB00011B/2695